George and Audrey

To Dick
with check...
George Witherwick

George Witherwick

"FANGS"

The Memoirs of a Gardening Dentist

Preface by
Elizabeth, Viscountess Falmouth

All proceeds from sales of this book will be
donated to the Royal Air Force Benevolent Fund

First published 1993

© George T. Witherwick 1993

A CIP catalogue for this book is available from the British Library.

ISBN 187344313 7

Published by the Author in association with
Landfall Publications,
Landfall, Penpol, Devoran, Truro, Cornwall.

Typeset and printed by the Troutbeck Press
and bound by R.Booth Ltd., Antron Hill, Mabe, Penryn, Cornwall.

CONTENTS

ACKNOWLEDGEMENTS

My sincere thanks and gratitude to the following:
Jean Marcus for her material help and friendship; Charmain Pearson for her kind and generous time spent in typing; Jennifer Maker for her faith and material help in promotion and distribution; and the Rev. Trevor McCabe for his unswerving encouragement towards publication.

PREFACE

George Witherwick has established himself in our Cornish Countryside by making the most fascinating garden in his little Valley, Trelean, which runs down to the Helford River. He and his wife, Audrey, came to Cornwall 14 years ago complete with lorry loads of substantial plants removed from his Surrey Garden where he had been gardening for 30 years, while carrying on his professional life as a dentist.

I doubt if anyone has ever seen so many interesting plants in such a small garden - a steep sided wooded valley with views of the River between the trees. All the plants are very choice and some of them of his making - several very exciting Rhododendron hybrids for instance, which he has so generously dispersed amongst his many friends. He has been so generous too with his time in giving illustrated lectures and talks and always produces a small microcosm of some aspect of gardening for the Cornwall Garden Society's Annual Show - very often adding to it his little stuffed hedgehog.

All who read this fascinating book will recognise his enormous energy and enthusiasm and his great knowledge of plants. He has an eye for the beautiful and his grouping of trees to complement one another is masterly. He must have one of the best collections for autumn colour in the County and his little vegetable patch produces choice delicacies for his special visitors.

Let us hope someone will love and care for this fascinating little valley jammed full of exciting plants when George is no longer with us.

Elizabeth, Viscountess Falmouth

FOREWORD

George Witherwick has been a good friend and colleague for over fifty years. He has always been a man of strict moral principles which he has assiduously maintained throughout his life though not always to his advantage.

This autobiography mainly covers the two primary interests of his life, dentistry and gardening. His success in both these fields demonstrates his versatility. Some of his experiences make interesting, and at times, amusing reading. He describes a cure for a slipped disc which is both unique and hazardous and his horticultural acumen which has won him national recognition supplies much constructive advice to all who are interested in gardening.

Dr. J. L. Trainer, L.D.S., F.D.S., R.C.S. Edin., L.R.F.P.S. Glasg., L.R.C.S. Edin.

Chapter 1

IN THE BEGINNING

I was born in Hull, or more correctly, Kingston-upon-Hull, in 1912 - a year that saw the Miners' Strike, the sinking of the Titanic and the first Balkan War, among other momentous events prior to World War I.

My earliest recollection of the war is of being taken downstairs in my night-clothes with my sister Enid to stand on the path behind our house, known as "Overstrand", in Newland Park, to gaze up at a huge Zeppelin, one of several that slipped across the North Sea under cover of darkness to bomb the port with no regard for civilian casualties. To me the airship was an unforgettable sight, lit up by the lights of the gondola basket slung beneath it and in which I could clearly see the heads of its crew. As the anti-aircraft guns blazed, I could see the flashes and the shells streaking their way into the sky and exploding, while the people in the gondola heaved bombs over the side to fall on the packed houses below, before making off at a snail's pace across the sea.

All this must have been worrying for my father, in charge of the local volunteer defences, which were organised at the house in Beverley Road from which we had recently moved. For some time, the defence of Hull was entrusted to one solitary weapon, a realistic-looking gun, actually made of wood, that stood on Wilberforce Bridge. With the arrival of the real guns, a battery of which was positioned in a field close by our house, came an unexpected drawback. The blast was too much for the front windows. Unlike the Zeppelin, which appeared in my young eyes to survive intact a shell that hit one side and came out at the other, our windows did not. After re-glazing them for the third time, father admitted defeat and boarded them up, and so they remained for the duration.

The night we were "hit" is still fresh in my mind. In complete darkness my father had opened the door of the bedroom I shared with

Enid, who bossed me with all the authority of her six-year seniority. "Come along, you two," he called. "Zeppelin raid!"

We scrambled out of the double bed and I grabbed the first combinations I could find and started to haul them on. My sister did likewise, only to find them much too small. She made a grab for mine, starting a chase that took us across the room, under the bed and over it, until I managed to get through the door and on to the landing, all in the dark. Then, I crawled backwards down the stairs and found sanctuary with my parents in the dining room, under the table. The silence that followed was broken by a series of heavy thumps that reverberated through the house.

"We've been hit!" screamed my mother. "Fred, we've been hit!"

On being urged to investigate, my father felt his way into the hall, fell over something at the foot of the stairs, crashed his head against the kitchen door, and let out a rich string of expletives. My mother, unused to such language, told him off in no uncertain manner, more concerned with the damage done to her precious little son's ears by the blasphemies than the physical harm to her daughter. That unfortunate girl had fallen headlong down the stairs in the black-out with a noise like bombs going off, and now lay in a moaning, blubbering heap. Amazingly, she suffered no serious injury.

I should mention here that my father and mother were, in that now rarely-used phrase, God-fearing people. Father played a leading role in the running of the local chapel, to which he devoted most of every Sunday, so my sister and I had a clear idea of moral values, rights and wrongs, from an early age. That teaching did little to dampen my natural high spirits, and I found myself in many a scrape, particularly in company with my bosom pal, John Leech, who also lived in Newland Park. What inhibited me more was a series of problems affecting my chest. Looking back, those early years appear as a constant struggle against illness; colds and coughs, bronchitis, the excruciating pain of pleurisy whenever I inhaled; all made worse by the pervasive dampness for which Hull was renowned.

My first remembered experience of medical treatment was during 1917 at the age of five, when I was taken into the big double bed in my parents' bedroom and told to sleep. I pretended to do so, but could not keep silent for long. When I shouted for my breakfast, I was reminded that there would be none for me that day. Around mid-morning, two men in black suits, carrying small Gladstone bags, came in and shut the door. They took off their coats, murmuring to each other in words I could not catch from by bolt upright alertness in the bed. Then one approached me with one hand behind his back.

"I'm going to place a mask on your face, laddie," he said with quiet authority. "You must be a good boy and breathe deeply." With this he put his free arm around me, and with the other, clamped a muslin mask over my face. The mask smelt awful from the chloroform that had been dripped on to it and which threatened to choke me as I took breath. I wriggled and tried to move my head away, but I was held fast. Frightened by the fear of choking, I found new strength, and managed to tear the mask from my face. I threw it across the room and jumped out of bed, but my visitors had seen it all before. I was quickly recaptured, held down, and the hated mask repositioned. Some time later I woke up to find the deed done. My tonsils and adenoids had been removed.

A year or two later, my second confrontation with medical practice occurred. A severe pain in my ear, the cause of which I knew only too well, woke me up one morning. I had previously been treated for a milder ear infection and been advised by the family doctor not to swim at the local baths; advice that had fallen upon unresponsive ears. Now I was being punished in a way that really hurt. My parents were attending some auction sale in the country, sister Enid was at boarding school, and I was alone with a pain that worsened every minute. Something had to be done.

In a moment of desperation I jumped on to my bike and cycled like mad into the city centre some three miles away. Here I found my way to Albion Street (the Harley Street of Hull), and in great trepidation rang the bell of the Ear, Nose & Throat Specialists, Drs. Rodger & Simpson. Between them they diagnosed a boil (otitis media, nowadays treated by antibiotics), bade me go home to await them, and turned up at lunchtime to commandeer the kitchen table, much to the indignation of Ethel our cook. This time I submitted to the chloroform mask, the boil was lanced, and the pain quickly receded.

My first experience of dentists came at about the age of eleven, when my father took me to his own practitioner, an elderly man who had learned his craft by being articled to a practising dentist, and who had not completed the intensive professional training that I was later to enjoy at Edinburgh. My problem was straightforward, as I now know - decay in a lower right molar that needed cleaning out and filling. Nonetheless this man decided to extract it, and as a

13

preliminary, gave me an extremely painful injection. It had been bad enough to see him fumbling with positioning the needle, but a good deal worse when he endeavoured to pull out the tooth with his forceps. Waves of pain shot through my jaw as he pushed the tooth this way and that, finally desisting to sit down. Even at my tender age it was obvious that the poor old chap was almost exhausted, and my pain was giving way to sympathy.

When battle was resumed after perhaps fifteen minutes, I wondered how much more I could stand. But the interval had given the injection time to work properly, and the agony was not repeated. A final wrench and the tooth gave up its tenacious hold, sending its adversary back to his chair panting for breath and looking quite exhausted.

Discussing it later, my father was sympathetic. "Yes," he agreed, "the man is getting too old to practise, but he has to go on."

"Why?" I wanted to know. "Why doesn't he stop?"

"Because he can't afford to. Like me, he's self-employed. Fishmongers and dentists are in the same boat there. Nobody pays us wages or a salary or a pension when we reach a certain age. We have to carry on until we can work no more, and hope our savings will tide us over the rest of our days."

I often recalled those words in later life.

Earlier I mentioned the Zeppelins, which loomed so large in my memory. Other events stand out that have a place here, and I suppose it was towards the end of the 1914-1918 War that the "feeding of the five thousand," as I like to term it, occurred. On that particular day I became aware of a crowd of people on the pavement outside. Investigation showed that the whole of Newland Park was thronged with women and children, the mothers wheeling prams loaded with all sorts of personal possessions. They spilled over on to the road and filtered into the adjoining playing fields, then used by Hull City Football Club Second Eleven.

On being alerted to this phenomenon, my mother rushed out to see for herself, followed by sister Enid, our cook and housemaid, and William the odd-job man. Mother at once organised a massive relief, running back and forth with cups of tea while cook produced endless buns and scones in the kitchen from a kind of treadmill. Luckily the gas stove or range was up to the job. Replete with big brass taps and an oven in which a 35lb turkey would look rather lost, it kept up its work until the late afternoon, when at last came word that the

Germans had not landed at Scarborough and were not marching on Hull. What had started it all was the gunfire from German ships that had raced across the North Sea, to shell Scarborough before nipping back to port. The rumour-mongers had got it wrong again.

Armistice Day was notable for the fact of my father being at home on a working day. I can see him now in his best suit, standing in front of the fire in the drawing-room, a fire that blazed with the brilliant flame of the incomparable Derby Brights, the best coal available at £5 for five tons that poorer people could not afford. A gold hunter watch and chain adorned his waistcoat, having at one end of the chain a gold sovereign case that always fascinated me. You pressed one side to reveal a full sovereign and the other for a half-sovereign. What my father said as he gestured benevolently with his cigar I cannot remember, but Armistice Day was clearly a special occasion.

Even after the War there were few motor cars on the roads, although my father's fishmongering business apparently ran to the expense of one, and to a large garage at the house with a smooth concrete floor ideal for spinning toys. Here, with my friend John Leech, we spent many a happy hour, whipping our tops from one side to the other, each of us a self-declared champion.

Stamp collecting, with Sister Enid supervising to ensure we didn't cheat each other on 'swops', was a regular winter occupation. It made a change from watching the Hornby train set showing its paces over a track that occupied almost the whole upstairs floor of 'Overstrand'. But nothing could beat the summer games, and a great favourite involved cutting very sharp points on three-foot bamboo sticks, ready to receive a walnut-sized 'cartridge' of heavy, sticky, moulded clay, into which a special-sized pebble was placed. Impaled on the point of the stick, this 'Mills bomb' as we named it was fired by a whipped swing that sent the missile huge distances. The advantage was that we could play it in the orchard in relative freedom from local damage. At least, so we thought until an extra good shot of mine disappeared in the direction of the house. Shortly after, my father called me in. I could tell from his face that I was in trouble, and when he got me into the drawing-room I could see why. Unbeknown to John and me, my projectile had sailed through the top of the bay window, shedding glass all over the carpet. Useless for me to deny my involvement. On the carpet in this Holy of Holies lay the incontrovertible evidence, the tell-tale stone. Needless to say, that most entertaining and original game came to a sudden end.

There were other days when games palled and adventure beckoned. One such was occasioned by the new bicycles we had been given and which represented a giant leap towards independence. The imposed condition - to stay in and around Newland Park and on no account to venture into the main road - seemed to limit that independence too severely. The urge to visit Mrs. Mallinson's shop across the high road to indulge ourselves with her lovely twopenny cones piled high with yellow ice-cream was too strong to ignore on a hot summer's day.

We set out together and reached the busy highway without incident. Here the trams clanked along their metal tracks, presenting a hazard I had not allowed for. Nobody had told me that the gaps between the polished metal shoulder of tramlines were wide enough to accept the wheel of a bicycle travelling along them. So although I joined the main road comfortably ahead of the approaching tram, I had not developed the technique of crossing the metals. When I needed to turn right further along, I found my front wheel seized by the tramline. It just would not let go, and after some moments of wobbling dangerously, I fell off, only yards in front of the tram.

Even today I can hear the screech of tortured metal as the driver, who surely deserved a medal for his prompt action, applied the brakes hard. The next moment, the "cow-catcher" he had simultaneously lowered scooped up the bike and its terrified owner, carrying both further along Cottingham Road, to where a bridge crossed the roadside dyke. Here the tram stopped, the conductor got out to retrieve me and my mangled bike from the "cow-catcher," and carried me across the bridge to a house where I was laid on a couch to be ministered to by a bevy of anxious women. Questions were asked, my parents informed by telephone, and I was taken home apparently none the worse for my experience, along with the remains of my bike. Needless to say, there were the inevitable lectures, and for some time to come, I was bikeless.

Thinking of tramlines reminds me of an amusing incident one Christmas. It was our custom to go to my Grandmother's on Christmas Day for the seasonal turkeys and, naturally, to receive presents from her and the other assembled relatives. On this occasion, it was snowing, and we all huddled into the Hansom cab that clip-clopped along for most of the way without incident.

Mother was decked out in a brand new outfit,mainly to outsmart her sister Nellie Newton who was always present. Mother was most concerned to arrive looking at her best, and well she might have done had it not been for the cab-driver's manoeuvre in overtaking a stationary conveyance, taking the cab to the middle of the road and getting the wheels wedged in the tramlines. My father called us all out to reduce the weight on the wheels, but mother refused. She was not going to get her feet and clothes wet in all that snow and slush. Everybody but mother then began to push and shove, but the wheels remained locked.

Father was getting cross by now, and insisted that my mother climb down, or we should never get the vehicle moving. With great reluctance, and watched by a small group of people on the pavement, she did so.

The further lightening of the weight on the wheels and everybody's renewed efforts did the trick. The wheels were freed, and we all clambered back on board to proceed on our way.

This should have been the end of the matter, but mother's hackles were up, and she started on my father. It was his fault for choosing a half-witted cabby, his fault that her shoes and dress were covered in muddy slush, and the moment we reached Grandmother's he must telephone for a different cabby.

We had never heard her berate father like this. Squeezed onto the back seat with me, Enid thought it all very funny and began to titter, at which mother fetched her a resounding clout on the head.

Mother continued her verbal onslaught against my father, who I was beginning to feel sorry for. The more he protested, the wilder became her accusations. Now it was her whole outfit that was ruined, and goodness knows what sister Nellie would think about it all.

The moment we arrived at Grandmother's, mother carried out her threat. Father had to use the telephone in the hall to order a different cabby to take us home, while mother stood over him. Only then was she satisfied, and took herself upstairs with my aunt Dinah to repair the damage, while Enid and I sought out aunt Sally, my favourite, in the back kitchen to whom in fits of laughter we related the sorry tale.

Grandma Mackinder, whose ancestors were offshoots of one of Scotland's largest and best-known clans, was to me the epitome of a prim and proper person. She would sit very upright in her wing chair, her small figure clothed from neck to toe in a black bodice and skirt, the bodice tight-fitting and laced with sequins and buttons, and having a small, fringed collar, also in black. From a case fixed to her bodice dangled pince-nez spectacles, the use of which gave her an even more severe demeanour. She did not take kindly to the episode which I shall now relate.

On that Christmas I was presented with a bow-and-arrow set. Mother had insisted to father that I was only to use it under his supervision, and not until we got home. However, after the Christmas feast when all had retired to the sitting-room to sleep it off, I crept from the room with Enid, intent on trying out this wonderful new plaything. In the back garden I soon got the hang of it, and to show my sister just how good I was, I proposed shooting an arrow right over the house into the front garden.

At about the third attempt I succeeded, the arrow sailing clean over the top of the house. I was still showing off to Enid, who seemed unable to use it herself, lacking the strength to bend the bow sufficiently, when the back door opened with my father shouting at me to bring the bow and arrows to him at once. I did so reluctantly, whereupon he seized it from me and proceeded to crack bow and arrows across his knee, ordering us back into the house. In the sitting-room, where all were now awake, there was an atmosphere you could have cut with a knife. I watched in horror as my father threw the pieces of my precious toy into the blazing fire before rounding on me for nearly killing a baby in a pram. While I listened open-mouthed, he told me that the arrow I had so innocently shot over the house had landed on a baby's pram being pushed along the pavement by the mother. The arrow had pierced the canvas cover, fortunately for me without injuring the baby inside. The outraged mother had promptly banged on the door to deliver an angry lecture to my father.

When father had finished, mother started on him. I had been told not to use the dangerous thing, but his was the greater sin. He should have prevented me, etc., etc. As if the destruction of my beloved toy were not enough, I was to go without my tea.

Unlike many men, I remember my childhood and school days with pleasure. I had none of the psychological hang-ups so often encountered today. Ours was a sensible household of what was then the lower-middle class. An example of my father's enlightened approach to his only son was when I was caught leaving the house with some of my own clothes to give to a beggar who had accosted me in the street nearby. It was not the first time I had been moved to do so by tales of poverty and woe; merely the first time I had been caught. My mother, barring the way to the front door, demanded to know what I intended to do with the suit over my arm. Under the barrage of questions I blurted out the truth, dodged past her, and ran off to where this down-and-out was sitting on the pavement, propped up against a garden fence, cigarette in mouth. I thrust the suit into his lap, ran back into the house and locked myself in the bedroom, refusing to let my mother enter.

I dreaded father's return that evening, and when opening the door to him, expected a good whacking from the strap that was his ultimate recourse. Instead, he sat on the bed with me and talked in a man-to-man fashion about the divisions of rich and poor; why some people succeeded and others didn't; some born to money, most having to work hard, simply to exist. It was a lesson that demonstrated its own proof later in my life.

As in other families, most activities centred on the kitchen. Ours was in charge of Ethel, fortyish and stout with arms like young trees, who hailed from a farm out towards Spurn in Holderness. The housemaid, Elizabeth, I cannot recall so well, but the memory of Monday wash-day, when they toiled together in their oiled aprons and flat caps, will always be with me.

Father had got a builder to construct a purpose-made wash-house on the rear east wall, a lean-to of brick under a slate roof. Here also was the pantry, coalhouse and outside WC, a superior place with the latest flushing arrangements and a nice, warm, welcoming wooden seat with brass fittings. The wash-house was large enough to have housed a medium-sized modern car, and promptly at 7 a.m. on the Monday, William our odd-job man would arrive to light the boiler and fill the copper with water. He would then set out all the wooden tubs and troughs, wash down the rollers of the big wringer, check and oil the cogs and handle. The dolly was unhooked from its place under the sloping roof, duck-boards set out in front of the two long tubs, and all was ready for the hot and steaming work to come.

Summer holidays until I was about seven were spent at Bridlington, where the one outstanding memory is of floating peacefully out to sea on the tide. My mother's foresight had ensured that I was dressed to survive practically anything my adventurous nature could lead me into. This "survival suit" was a lightweight but cumbersome, all-in-one affair of vivid yellow oilskin, or similar, gathered at cuffs and ankles with elastic and fastened lightly at the neck. My nurse kept watch from a deck-chair, knitting and chattering nineteen to the dozen to another such. On the day in question, my parents were not in evidence, and nobody at first saw a small boy lying on his back in the sea, being carried further and further out. My story might have ended there, as on several occasions since, but for the vigilance of an unknown observer. I was rescued from deep water in the nick of time.

A more exciting experience awaited me one day in Bridlington. I had accompanied my father to the main Post Office which contained a telephone kiosk. We somehow squeezed into it while he made a telephone call to his secretary, Miss Constance Bloom, who ran the business in Hull during his absence. He was speaking to her when an almighty bang came over the line, so loud that he fell back against the door, pushing us both out and leaving the receiver dangling by its cord. When he had gathered his wits, my father grabbed the telephone and shouted: "Miss Bloom! What is it?"

There was no reply. He shouted again and again, obviously fearing the worst. At long last we heard Miss Bloom's excited voice. "It's blown up."

"What has? What's blown up?"

"The airship," came the answer. "The R38. It's coming down in flames."

All this coming out of the phone in a high-pitched scream brought everybody in the Post Office to a standstill, agog for more news. Next day, the story broke in banner headlines in all the Nationals, which with the rare crystal sets used to receive radio transmissions were the only means of mass communication then.

About 1919, the family including the maids began spending the last three weeks of August and the first week in September at Scarborough, some forty miles north of Hull. Scarborough was the queen of watering places then, and had much more to offer than Bridlington. I quickly made friends with a couple of local lads, day-boys at the prestigious Scarborough College, Frank and Midge Horsley. And what times we had! Armed with stout iron shovels, we soon changed the contours of the beach with our "sand-works", particularly at the south cliffs, just below the cliff railway. Here we laboured mightily, racing against the incoming tide to create "dug-outs" fully three feet wide at the base and tapering to perhaps a third of that at a height of ten feet. It never occurred to us, as water swirled about our feet, that the sea could undermine our careful work while in progress and bury us all under tons of damp sand. It was here, showing off our prowess in the sea that I developed the interest that later resulted in my becoming a school captain of swimming.

Before going on with my story, I must hark back once more to that magical age of seven years old. Why? A number of events in that first post-World War I year seem to have begun a trend that shaped my life thereafter, and none more so than my very first garden. My interest in plants must have been very evident for my father had noticed that on Saturday afternoons I could often be found helping William at his work of tending the extensive garden behind the house, which had a lawn large enough to play tennis on, and on which could be seen billowing long lines of washing on a Monday morning. There were also flower beds, an orchard, some ornamental trees, and of course a vegetable plot.

One weekend, father took me aside. "I see you've been helping William in the garden," he said. "How would you like one of your own, to do whatever you liked with?"

I jumped at the chance, and he was as good as his word. A plot of earth some two yards square in area became mine, thereby awakening a passion that was to fascinate, perplex, absorb and enchant me for more than seventy years.

John Leech shared my good fortune in having a father similarly indulgent, and boys being boys, we had to compete for the best results. It was an opportunity to set forth on our bikes to scour the nearby countryside for new little seedling trees which could be transplanted in our respective plots. Flowers we had no interest in. Only girls and cissies went in for flowers. Trees were different - so full of growing power, so manly. An old chalk-pit on the road from Cottingham to Beverley, at the bottom of a steep hill overlooked by a farmhouse, held a plentiful supply of saplings in its overgrown wastes, and this became our favourite venue. Gradually we began to see the results of our transplantations, some successful, others not, just as it always has been. This hobby we fitted in with all the other activities to be expected from boys in the "Just William" mould so beautifully created by Richmal Crompton and now virtually forgotten. Riding bikes "no hands", birds nesting, knocking tins off posts with catapults, bashing hell out of conkers, having enormous bonfires on Guy Fawkes night, those were the things that mattered. When we eventually took stock of our little gardens and totted up the trees we had each grown, I was thrilled with the result: Leech, ten species; Witherwick, fourteen species. It gave me a satisfaction unlike anything I had experienced before.

John Leech was also a part of my school life when I transferred from the Hull Girls High School to Hymers College. Others I remember were Kenneth Hibbert, the Zerneys, Jack and Russell Young, and an awful master called Griffiths, though he was balanced somewhat by a very nice woman teacher, Miss Skinner. I was there long enough to win a Hymers College Cap for appearing in the under twelves Cricket Eleven (the cap still fits me today!) before the next move on. This was of sufficient importance to be the subject of the next chapter.

Chapter 2

TEENAGE - SCARBOROUGH - LONDON 1926

At the age of fourteen, I became a pupil at Scarborough College, a very different scene from the school I had left. The College had a high academic reputation under its headmaster Percy Armstrong, a cousin of Rudyard Kipling, whom he resembled strongly in appearance and character. Laurence Armstrong, a brother who ran the Prep school, assisted also with the running of the College. I came to love the school, with all it stood for, and I can truthfully say that some of the very happiest days of my life were spent there.

My going to Scarborough was largely due to the wisdom of our family GP, Dr. Briggs of Sunny Bank. In those days, doctors had much more incentive than today to keep a close check on their 'panel' patients, and Dr. Briggs was a thoroughly conscientious practitioner. He suggested to my parents that the damp atmosphere of Hull was not good for a lad with persistent bronchial trouble. Why not try Scarborough? Its climate was so much more bracing.

The decision turned out to be more far-reaching in its effects than anyone could have foreseen. I thrived in my new environment and developed an interest in sport that later gave me the great satisfaction of captaining my House and the school side at every game played. Nor did being away from my parents bother me much. Although I had a comfortable home, it was very grown-up to be away, and I enjoyed it to the full.

My first term, easter 1926, got off to an exciting start. I was in the west dormitory, next to the Headmaster's flat, when at 4.30 a.m. I was awakened by a most curious sensation. The bed was waltzing about the floor, as were those of the other boys, accompanied by a furious rattling as everything shook. We were excited and frightened, but the tremors lasted only a few seconds and did not endanger anybody. We were not surprised to learn at breakfast that a rare and fortunately minor earthquake had been recorded over a wide area.

Something must have upset the elements that year, for not content with an earthquake, we had a typhoon, witnessed by me from the big window in the main schoolroom. It began as the gathering of a big, black cloud at the end of the long valley leading to Seaton. Gradually from this menacing dark mass, a spout formed, twisting and turning down to the ground, looking for all the world like an elephant's trunk, all the time coming along the valley towards the school. Then the wind struck us, growing every minute in intensity until it was a roaring hurricane followed by lashing rain. While I watched, the wind wreaked havoc with anything not securely tied down. Haystacks, sheds, small trees, slates, even goal-posts and nets, all hurtled through the air or were bundled along the first eleven soccer pitch. It was all over in the space of perhaps ten minutes, and in that time the wind had stripped the tiles and slates from many of the surrounding roofs, giving us several days' work in clearing the football pitches of debris.

My first year at Scarborough was also to mark the second visit to a dentist. For days and nights I had suffered agony from toothache. With vivid memories of my earlier experience I tried to ignore it, but of course it did not go away. After one sleepless night crying with the pain, I gave in and reported to the Headmaster, who promptly got me an appointment with a dentist whose surgery was close to the Cambridge Hotel in Scarborough.

Here I experienced very different treatment. I hardly felt the anaesthetising needle, where the other man had fumbled and jabbed, and the tooth was out before I had realised it. The relief was enormous, and on the way back to school I felt like singing aloud. The difference between the two men was something that I remembered later when choosing a career. The Scarborough man was a Surgeon Dentist, with qualifications proudly displayed on the brass plate on his surgery wall. The other had no recognised qualification at all.

Alleviating the grind of school-work, at which I performed adequately, was the companionship of other lads and - briefly - the other sex. I was reminded of this recently when reading Ludovic

Kennedy's autobiography - the episode describing his love at fifteen for a master's wife at Eton. Mine was for Nurse Wilkinson, a sweet, bouncy, plump little piece of femininity. She was an SRN from Leeds, called in by the school when an epidemic of German Measles and fever overwhelmed poor matron and her assistant. Nurse Wilkinson coped splendidly with the situation, and I found myself attracted to her. I was then about seventeen, a House Captain and School Prefect, and considered myself quite a fellow.

Her bedroom, as I soon discovered, was reached from a flight of stairs that led to two rooms and a dormitory (of which I was the Monitor), below the clock tower. The bedroom was directly above that of the Physics Master, Mr. Batey, who could not have been unaware of my comings and goings but said not a word. Night after night, in pyjamas and dressing-gown, Nurse Wilkinson and I would sit on each other's laps whispering sweet nothings. In this way we passed many pleasant hours, I with my hand on her bosom, she innocently holding nothing more than my other hand. For the three weeks or so that it lasted, nobody in the school had any inkling of it

Another enjoyable though very different pleasure that year, was the school trip to Belgium and Holland. Led and organised by the Rev. Beech, whose son was a contemporary of mine at college, becoming Head Boy and latterly a vicar, its purpose was to show us the cemeteries, monuments and landmarks of World War I. There were about fourteen of us as I remember, and I shared a room in a Blankenburg Hotel with a friend from Huddersfield, Dick Booth. Dick and I distinguished ourselves by getting lost in Brussels, a particularly silly mishap in view of the fact that we hardly spoke a word of Flemish, French or German. Nonetheless, we managed to convey our plight to the local people, and having done so, were amazed at the unstinting help offered. One dedicated taximan almost killed us all in his enthusiasm, driving us at breakneck speed through the city traffic from one station to another in search of our party, which by a miracle we found in time. I shall always be grateful for the kindness extended to us in those balmy days before the Second World War. I do not think a pair of English youths in that predicament today would have such a friendly reception, when the behaviour of our 'lager louts' abroad has soured the better feelings of many continentals.

The one jarring incident in the otherwise happy recollection of those times concerns the General Strike of 1926. During the Easter holidays I happened to be outside Blundells Paint Factory in Hull, at the corner of Beverley Road. With my father and two of his employees we watched a group of men stop one of the Corporation trams, which were being run mainly by volunteers from Cambridge University. When everyone had dismounted, the striking Union men tried manually to push the tram off its rails, but of course it was too heavy. Half a dozen men were then sent into the factory, shortly to return armed with six foot long iron posts. These they arranged under the chassis of the tram and proceeded to use them as levers. The tram rocked to and fro with increasing violence until one last mighty heave pushed it beyond the point of balance, and over it went, to crash with a tremendous impact on the ground. The wreckage blocked half the road, and my father turned away in disgust. "Now you have seen the rise of a new unelected power in England," he commented bitterly.

During the summer holidays that year, my father took us to London for the Wembley Exhibition. We set off in his car, a Moon, the latest open model with hood, running boards, a rubber bulb horn and wheels with fine wire spokes radiating from the hubs. Across the back was the petrol tank, where also was located the spare wheel. There was an internal pull-out celluloid windscreen for those in the rear, and when the hood was up the sides were open to the weather. My mother, Enid and I sat in the back, suitably attired in leather motoring coats, light orange in colour. We had travelling rugs across our knees, and mother's hat was secured firmly beneath her chin with a strap. Father occupied the front seat alongside the chauffeur, an alert, fussy young employee by the name of Sutton who was supposed to understand all about automobiles.

For me the big thrill was when we hit the Great North Road at Boroughbridge. The road was the premier highway of England, and its four hundred mile route from London to Edinburgh held all the glamour of unknown places crying out to be explored.

I was surprised by the few vehicles on the road, and soon learned that an unspoken code of conduct was observed. When we wished to overtake another vehicle, travelling at perhaps thirty or forty miles per hour, our driver would hoot. The other driver would slow down, wave us on with arm fully extended, and we would go by. At the moment of passing, both drivers would raise their hats, incline their heads, or otherwise acknowledge. When meeting an oncoming car, each driver would slow down to about fifteen miles an hour, the usual courtesies would be exchanged, and so we proceeded.

We stopped about every hour on our journey, whereupon Sutton would climb down to examine the tyres, feel the temperature of the wheel hubs in case the brakes had been binding or a bearing was running hot, and raise the bonnet to let the engine cool. Tyre pressures were carefully checked, and a glance underneath the body would spot any unwanted dripping of oil. Stops were usually organised in the forecourts of hotels so that the ladies could powder their noses while the men had a quiet smoke.

The traffic had begun to thicken at Baldock, and from Hatfield into the centre of London it was so dense I was flabbergasted. Everywhere I looked, on every side, were cars, omnibuses, horse-drawn vehicles, trams, all clanking, roaring or hooting and rushing somewhere in a desperate hurry. At the Berners Hotel, just off The Strand, we created something of a sensation in our open car and brightly coloured leather coats. We were clearly the country cousins, forsaking the haymaking for the city lights.

We were due to spend four days in London, booked in at the Berners Hotel, and we certainly made every moment count. At the Wembley Exhibition, I begged to be allowed on the giant switchback. My mother refused to let Enid go, but conceded reluctantly to father's offer to ride on it with me. It was quite terrifying, and the moment I stepped off the thing, I was as sick as a dog, laughing and crying at the same time while poor father caught the sharp edge of mother's tongue for upsetting her son so!

Our schedule included a visit to the Palladium, where Harry Tate's fishing sketch had me 'rolling in the aisle' with laughter, but the greatest thrill of all came after watching the Changing of the Guard at St. James Palace. My father very bravely led us into the Palace stable yard. We stood looking across the yard at the front door of St. James's when into the cobbled yard stole an immense Daimler car, the biggest I had ever seen, and pulled up opposite the front door. To our great delight, out stepped the King, Queen Mary and the Prince of Wales. The car pulled away, the Royal party moved towards the door, then turned as one to face us. Father raised his hat and bowed, mother with her fox fur draped around her neck dropped a curtsy, while I just stood agape. The King touched his top hat with his stick, Queen Mary raised her arm in her gracious wave, followed by the Prince of Wales. Then they turned and went into the Palace, leaving us alone in the yard and mother reduced to tears by the unexpected joy of a unique experience.

As will be seen, my mother was an emotional person, easily moved by events - a characteristic I have inherited. She was also very proper in everything she did, and loved order and routine. Whenever I returned home for holidays from Scarborough College, I noticed that nothing had changed. Washday was still Monday, with the ironing done in the evening and the maid heating the heavy flat-iron on the kitchen range. Thursday was reserved for turning out the dining-room, requiring us to take lunch and high tea in the hall, an area more spacious than in most modern homes, that must have been eighteen feet by fifteen overall. Sundays were reserved for Chapel-going, the traditional roast, and the winding of the various clocks, the settings of which were carefully checked by father with his gold Hunter watch that must have kept impeccable time.

My mother was always beautifully dressed and with never a hair out of place, - the result no doubt of her twice-weekly visit to the hairdresser. The untidiness she saw in me as a boy must have annoyed her as much as it did my father, who on checking his appearance in the hall mirror before going out one day, surveyed me with some displeasure. "Both your mother and I know you're not very smart," he told me, "but there's no need for you to step outside for everyone else to know it by your dishevelled appearance."

In later years I took a lot more care.

Mother's meticulousness extended to such activities as the making of tea. This had to be done only in a silver teapot. Other types lost heat quicker or dripped at the spout she said. One caddy-spoon of tea per person and one for the pot, no more and no less, was put into the pre-heated pot, the boiling water poured on, and the Ceylon tea given four or five minutes to infuse before the first cup was drawn. Then, each cup with its correct amount of milk was half-filled in turn, to be topped up on the second pouring. If the procedure seemed tedious, at least the taste of the tea was beyond reproach.

It was as well that my mother enjoyed the running of a house and the entertaining. Most Sundays we had a parson to lunch, who sometimes stayed over the weekend, as befitted father's status as Secretary to the Wesleyan Chapel Council, on which he served for no less than 26 years. Little did we know at the time that one of these parsons began to form a little clique opposed to father, with a view to undermining his position. The movement gathered strength until at last he was forced to resign. I was not then aware that this episode typified the in-fighting that goes on in committees in every walk of life, where the good and conscientious are frequently ousted by those more ruthless in their greed for power. My father, whose social life was inseparable from the Chapel, took it very badly. On one occasion he said to me: "Never get involved with politics, son, or local committees, or any council, unless you want to get stabbed in the back by your colleagues." This from a good man, whose almost single-handed efforts had raised the fund to build Cottingham Road Wesleyan Chapel, and who after Chapel service every Sunday would take me with him on tour of the new site, reporting progress to the Clerk of Works on the Monday morning, all in his own unpaid time.

To return to Scarborough College, the year 1928 brought a great freeze, such as we have had in England only a few times since. For six weeks or more the ground was frozen below the layer of snow, and many local sheets of water iced over thickly enough to skate on. What a chance for some winter sports! I was very friendly at the time with some day-boys, Guy and Titch Horsley and their family, and between us we knocked up a huge bob-sledge. Built of one-inch thick timber, it had a separate, articulated steering unit swivelling at the front for the driver, who steered by using his legs on the two side projections. We took it to the far side of Oliver's Mount, where a very large grass field, covered with snow, had a ridge with an eight foot drop. The problem was that in making the sledge so strong, we had also made it so heavy that at the end of each run, it took all five of us three-quarters of an hour to toil back up the slope. It was worth any effort, though. On starting off, the rear two would run with the sledge to push me off and jump on as it gathered momentum. At the ridge, we became airborne, and provided we landed right side up, we continued at a tremendous rate, perhaps forty miles an hour, to the bottom, where trees and a hawthorn hedge formed the boundary. Avoiding miraculously the tree trunks, we smashed through the hedge, down a steep bank and on to the road that ran from St. Margaret's Girls School to the Mere. With luck the sledge's momentum would carry us all the way to the Mere, a total distance of about half-a-mile.

On Sundays, the main day for this activity, the road to the Mere was busy with people taking their Sunday stroll. The sight of the huge sledge with five boys in football gear shouting and screaming their heads off was enough to persuade any pedestrian to give way, and nobody was injured.

A rather less strenuous pastime than hauling the heavy sledge up the slopes was learning to ice-skate. I borrowed a pair of skates, and helped by some earlier experience with roller-skating, found it not too difficult. While the extreme cold lasted, we had plenty of practice on a stretch of playground we flooded each night. It ran in a V-shape from the gymnasium to the school wall, and we would push ourselves off from the wall to skate back across the playground. Wonderful fun.

Quite a different kind of fun beckoned with the chance of a flight with Alan Cobham, whose flying circus we heard was coming to Scarborough. The problems were that the town itself was out of bounds, even on the Sunday we proposed, and the cost was 5/- each : that represented the total of my pocket-money for five weeks. I decided to go with a school-friend, "Kitty" Shaw, now Group Capt. R. H. Shaw (Retired), who shared my ambition to join the RAF on leaving school, but there was a further difficulty. We learned that the planes were to be parked at Scarborough racecourse, well north of the town, a distance as the crow flies of four or five miles. There was no transport, and we could not get away before lunch was over, having to be back again by 5 p.m., before we were discovered.

On the day, we set off at a run in our Marlborough suits with stiff white collars, and did not stop until we had reached the racecourse. Here we were very disappointed to have to join a huge queue waiting for the chance to take a flight. We waited and waited, and by the time four o'clock came we were loudly bemoaning our plight. As luck would have it, somebody in front of us took pity. He left his place to go to the head of the queue, where he found the man in charge and returned with him. "Come along, you lads," he said. "Follow me."

Happily at the head of the queue, we paid our 5/- and clambered up into the aircraft. It was a biplane and rather ancient, made of wood and apparently held together with string. This in no way detracted from the thrill as we took off. Our main disappointment was that the pilot did not fly over our school and land on the cricket pitch. That would have been perfect. As it was he flew us round the north side and back again to the racecourse, a flight of some seven minutes duration. Back on terra firma, we had no time to think about the experience before racing back to school the way we had come. When we arrived, we found that everybody had gone in to Sunday tea, which we were determined not to miss. By repeatedly tapping on the window, we managed to attract the attention of a boy who crawled across to the door to open it. We promptly followed him on all fours to our respective tables, unnoticed by the masters whose own table was set apart from the others.

Our escapade was a seven-day wonder in the College and we enjoyed the status of folk-heroes. A few years later, Kitty Shaw went into the RAF via Cranwell, while I had to wait until war was declared, in deference to my mother's unyielding objection.

My aptitude for field sports and swimming, coupled with a highly competitive nature, brought its rewards. During my last year at Scarborough College, I was captain of hockey and football and of most other games. In swimming, at which I delighted in showing off by diving from the topmost board and swimming underwater to the shallow end, I obtained my Life-saving Merit Medal and nobody could have guessed that this was the same boy whose weak chest had been a constant source of concern in Hull. I had proved that my lungs were as healthy as the next boy's and at the same time vindicated the stand of our family doctor in recommending a change of climate.

A few years on, I would regret my inattention in certain academic subjects, notably chemistry. The favourite diversion here was to blow down the bunsen burner while the teacher was explaining something to the others. My confederate in this was none other than a parson's son, Dudley Wright, and our innocent little trick caused the gaslights in the Headmaster's classroom to pop and hiss alarmingly. The idea probably originated with Dudley, whose yearning to experiment turned on one occasion to the use of acid, with which he proceeded to inscribe a message on my wrist. I still bear the mark he left, along with a bald patch on the head resulting from another of his bright ideas.

I continued to collect awards in that last year - House Captain, School Captain, second Head Prefect under Ticker Whittaker (later to become Sir John Whittaker), all came my way. I was also President of the Debating Society, Meteorological Officer, and in charge of the Museum. My eight stone six pound frame seemed to generate an inexhaustible energy. I even ventured into the realms of moral judgment when lecturing the school one memorable time on the 'Decline of morality,' a feat that Percy Armstrong, our founding headmaster, declared had not been attempted by any pupil in all his thirty years. On my last day at Scarborough College, after supper in the front hall, he asked me to wait while he went to his study. Returning, he pressed on me two volumes of Kipling, beautifully bound in leather. Inside the fly-leaf of each, he had written 'I shall miss you, Witherwick, but the school will miss you more.'

31

Chapter 3

ROYAL COLLEGE OF SURGEONS, EDINBURGH

If I imagined that prowess at school would automatically be followed by distinction in a career, I was to be disappointed. First, there was the difficult decision as to what path to follow. I knew already that I would not be joining my father in his fish, poultry and game business, nor did I wish to go into Chapel, although I taught at Sunday school for a while and swelled the numbers in my class. Plenty of other courses were open to me, but I kept coming back to my experiences with dentists at the ages of eleven and fourteen. It began to seem that being a good dentist was a worthwhile occupation. You had the means of saving people from continual pain, and that must be good in itself. Then there was the lure of professional status, like that of a doctor. After a lot of heart-searching, I decided I would train as a dentist.

The need for such a decision was not one I had been prepared for. All along I had assumed that I would follow my father into the business his own father had started. That would have provided a nice continuity. One Easter he had drawn me aside to discuss "a serious matter," as he put it. The upshot of it was that he had formed the opinion that his business was in a slow decline, and that in the future it might not provide a secure income for me and any dependents. Both he and my mother believed that I should be trained to enter some trade or profession involving an essential service that would not be subject to the swings and vagaries of the public's buying habits.

Needless to say, this 'bolt from the blue' set me back on my heels for a while. Knowing that my father was a shrewd and practical man did not help, and it was only on his death, years later, that I realised the value of his foresightedness. For now, I was stuck with having to revise all my ideas of a career, and began to wish that I had paid more attention to academic subjects than to excelling in sport. This was to be a constant theme when I considered all the hard work I would be obliged to undertake in pursuing a career in dentistry.

The decision pleased my father, who with his usual thoroughness looked at the best way in which I could achieve my aim. He had already advised me to choose something where, by my skill and training, I could be my own master, and not be beholden for my income to any individual, and certainly not the Government, for which he had nothing but scorn.

"What do you have against the Government?" I made bold to ask him.

"In my opinion, son," was his reply, "when Government steps into a business concern or industry through the front door, all honesty, responsibility and efficiency steps out of the back door."

In Easter 1928, he could not have known what effects the dead hand of the first post-World War Socialist Government would have throughout the country. That harsh judgment was unfortunately vindicated, as I found to my cost.

He had established that the best training for would-be dental surgeons was to be had at Edinburgh University, and about this he was adamant. Never mind the cost. Everything would be provided for as long as it took me to qualify. First I would need to matriculate (how lucky he did not realise my grave doubts about that ever happening!) Then I would need to pass the entrance examination. It was all quite clear to him.

It was not so clear to certain relatives when they heard. "Dentistry!" shrilled my aunt Dorothy, who had married a chemist and welcomed the opportunity to abuse my father. "What a waste of good money to put George to such a low and unrewarding profession."

To me she said later: "There are not many good dentists about. They're mostly butchers. What makes you think you're God's gift to suffering humanity?"

On hearing of this, my father sought to undo the damage caused by this piece of female venom. "Your aunt has personal reasons for her outburst against me," he reassured me. "Ignore it. I believe you have the right disposition to make a success. I've seen how you look after your piece of garden and care for the pigeons. I've promised to help you in every way I can, and you can rely upon that."

He was as good as his word. To his eternal credit, he provided the money to support me through the long years of training, which went on until I was twenty-six, not bringing a penny into the house in this period. There were no student grants then. However, as a true Yorkshireman he was not going to throw good money away on a lad who might feel faint when it came to the crunch, so when he saw I was keen, he arranged for me to be 'articled' to a well-known Dental Surgeon in Hull, ostensibly to learn dental mechanics in his workshop. In fact, I was to be fetched upstairs to the surgery whenever a general anaesthetic case was being dealt with. As soon as the patient was 'under,' I had to stand by the surgeon and watch him perform at close quarters. My response to the gory goings on was duly reported to my father, who could thereby satisfy himself that his son had the stomach for the job he had chosen.

I was fortunate in my father's choice of tutor. The surgeon went out of his way and beyond his contract to extend my experience. He would take me to people's homes in the outlying countryside, mostly in Holderness, also to nursing homes, and twice to the Hull Royal Infirmary. The time I spent under his care confirmed me in my resolution to take up dentistry, and had the practical advantage of replacing a whole year's study at Edinburgh University, whose entrance examination I duly passed with some surprise. My going to Edinburgh was a family event. Mother's role was to find suitable digs, father's to see the Dean of the Faculty. Sister Enid, who had been away at Penrose College while I was at Scarborough, had subsequently married a very nice man, Pearson Crabtree, and was not available to join us. The three of us set out from Hull that morning and arrived at Newcastle around 12.30 p.m., where we planned to have lunch at the five-star Turk's Head Hotel, which my father understood to be the best in Newcastle. Father and the driver of the Hudson car would park it and join us at the hotel. I was to take mother into the dining-room and book a table.

This magnificent hotel had an imposing entrance, and we went through swing doors to a very large lounge. We had not gone more than a few steps when a bedlam of noise hit us. Mother stopped in her tracks and turned pale. The room was full of swearing men in shirt sleeves and braces, collarless, and mostly very drunk. Some sprawled on the floor, others were seated, loudly debating in shouted volleys of four-letter words. A stench of lavatories hung over all. I led my mother outside, where she sank to the steps, asking repeatedly,

"Whatever is it? What's happening in there?"

I had never seen anything like it, and neither had father, who on joining us marched through the swing doors to investigate. He returned grim-faced, grabbed mother's arm and led her round the corner to a garage at the back of the hotel, just in time to catch the driver before he disappeared for his lunch.

We all got into the car and drove to a place called Morpeth, into the Courtyard of a lovely old coaching inn. Here we had lunch in very different surroundings from those of the Turk's Head. Only now did my father, more relaxed, speak of that experience. He had gone through the mélee into the dining-room to see the Head Waiter, who informed him that this was the final lunch before the T.U.C. members left the hotel. All week the conference had gone on in a series of drunken orgies, the men drinking until they could take no more and collapsed on the floor or slept on chairs. Bedrooms upstairs were used as latrines, female staff locked themselves in their rooms at night and refused to enter bedrooms for fear of molestation.

It is this scene that comes to mind today whenever I see the T.U.C. annual event reported on TV. Perhaps things have improved since then.

Scotland was not altogether foreign to me. Before going up to University we had spent a happy family holiday at the Peebles Hydro. There I learned to dance the Dashing White Sergeant, the Highland Fling and other Scottish dances, all helped no doubt by the dash of Scots blood in my veins. So with good digs, I settled down in my new environment.

In other circumstances I might have made more of the social life that all students, especially medical ones, are said to revel in. The fact is that shortly before leaving Hull, I had met Audrey, my future wife, through a mutual interest in badminton. It was at a club run by the 4th East Yorkshire Regiment at their barracks in Park Street, Hull. I had always thought badminton a silly game, but if playing it kept me close to Audrey, that was what I had to do. We got to know each other fairly well during the two or three evenings each week that we played, and soon 'plighted our troth,' as the saying goes. She must have been courageous to face the known prospect of my five or six years as an impecunious student, and fate was to make life even more difficult for us. Her father had a managerial position on the wholesale side of W.H. Smith, and shortly after we met, he was moved with his family to Cardiff. So our 'courting' was mostly by telephone and letter.

35

I threw myself into the University routine of lectures and hospital visits, determined to try for a Triple Qualification (as doctor and dentist). The two years I had spent with the dental surgeon in Hull had given me plenty of confidence that I could do the job once I had passed the exams. I was very interested in the surgical side, and spent more time in the hospital wards than the curriculum allowed. It was here that I met my Waterloo, clustered with others around the bed of a woman awaiting an abdominal operation while the consultant held forth on her probable ailment. I had caught her eye, and when the surgeon moved along, I spoke to her, trying to give her encouragement for her impending operation.

In due course we came upon her again. There she was, unconscious on the table in the operating theatre, with the surgeon pulling her organs about like wet fish on a monger's slab. Whether I was upset by his apparent callousness, or whether it was the thought of her warm smile when I spoke to her, I do not know to this day. But all at once my stomach revolted, and I was compelled to make a noisy and undignified exit, upsetting to all concerned.

The episode so affected me that I could not come to terms with it. For two days I did little more than roam the streets of Edinburgh, while trying to find a way to continue. In the end I had to accept my weakness for what it was, and came to the obvious conclusion. To be a successful surgeon, one has to see the patient simply as a body, and be able to work on it as such. To see it as an individual with personalty can only bring emotional involvement that will impair one's skill and lead to ultimate failure. Having realised that, I was content to leave general surgery to my betters, and make do with minor surgery to the head, neck and arms.

It was not long before I was a patient myself. I had been suffering from severe headaches, and when I decided to do something about it, my landlady got me an appointment with her own G.P.

"I see you've got some infection in the antrum at the side of your nose," he told me. "Go to the Out-patients Department at the Infirmary tomorrow morning and let them examine you."

I did so, and was quickly seen to. A white-coated gent examined me, I was ushered into a cubicle, and had the antrums washed out with a saline solution to neutralise the infection. The infection had caused inflammation of the small branch of the facial nerve which thereby gave me the terrible headaches. Known as a "Proof Puncture," this simple operation with a local anaesthetic had me on my way to the University within half an hour.

The long days of study were broken up by holidays, or vacations as they are now known, and these were spent with Audrey. A particularly memorable year was 1935, when together we visited Cornwall for the first time, in a hired car with her eldest brother Kenneth, who worked on a sheep farm in New Zealand.

All we did was to dash around looking at places and things, which was very agreeable. Out of the towns, it was peaceful and quiet, with nothing on the roads, not even tractors. Cornwall was then a very isolated county. One felt a sense of exploration, coupled with a feeling of distrust toward us by some of the natives, who were by no means forthcoming in reply to our questions. This insularity was especially noticed on the Lizard round Kuggar and on to Cadgwith. Passing through Ruan Minor we stopped and joined a small group standing in front of a wooden shed opposite the church, and on the counter were displayed numerous turned pieces of serpentine. Inside, a man of about thirty was in the process of demonstrating on his revolving wheel the art of turning this special stone found only on the far southerly tip of the Lizard peninsula. Most of what he had on show was of a lovely deep red colour, and the outstanding pieces were two ten inch candlesticks gleaming in the sunlight from their high polish. Whatever the price,which I forget, it was quite beyond our resources - in fact we bought nothing, but marvelled at the man's skill and tenacity, not only making the pieces but in trying to sell them to passing visitors. Little then did I realise that some thirty five years later I should meet up again with this man, Albert Williams, living at Poltesco.

At Cadgwith as we walked around we felt many eyes were upon us. It was not long before we were accosted by a Cornish lady intent on trying to interest me in buying a cottage sitting near to the top of the cove, and which in the end reduced itself in price to £50! In fact I had little more than fifty shillings. I was being coerced by this high-speed talkative Cornish woman, when my wife-to-be blandly informed me that the place, i.e. Cadgwith, was dirty and stunk of fish! Well, so it did, with rotting bits of it all over the place and the top of the beach covered in it. In those days Cornwall was full of fish at knock down prices, most of which was not sold and just chucked down for the taking, whether by humans, dogs or cats.

St. Ives was little better; nets and fish baskets all over the road by the beach and harbour and the fish market or auction, which took place on the slipway opposite the famous Sloop Inn. The market was a daily spectacle, attended by a good many of the local inhabitants and always by a man in a pony and trap, with a most attractive collie dog who followed the trap, tucked in underneath between the wheels, who then sat there while his master attended the sale. It was at St. Ives that we discovered an amazing secondhand shop, three quarters of the way down Fore Street on the left-hand side going towards the Sloop. The small frontage windows gave no hint of the massive size of the place behind, and what's more, having an upstairs walk-around gallery. Here I was so impressed with a stuffed hedgehog, resplendent in its oval glass dome and set on a nice wooden stand, that I bought it for 5/-d, and have it still. In this secondhand emporium was an amazing storehouse of just about anything and everything you could possibly think of, most of it Victorian. I nearly bought a pillar box with Victoria Regina stamped on it but the price of £1 was beyond me if we were to get back to Yorkshire.

However, I recall, also before we had stepped into this Aladdin's Cave of bygones, and which today would fetch thousands of pounds instead of the pence and shillings of 1935, we had halted at a small shop, also on the left-hand side of Fore Street, its windows plastered with handwritten notices and a photo of a hillside with sheep and a boy sitting on a rock. There was quite a crowd inside, and at the counter was a biggish woman who, between speaking *sotto voce* to those nearest, kept raising her voice and saying, "He was just minding the sheep and they took him." At the counter the lady was asking people to sign a petition, presumably to indicate their disapproval of this outrageous act whereby "they" just came and took "him" whilst he sat minding the sheep. The photo on the window depicted the peaceful rural scene - who "they" were I could not find out, nor "him," so I asked a question from the doorway but could not get the sense of what she said. For all I know it could have been in Cornish, and I had not the gall to ask anyone.

The whole episode at the time seemed peculiar to say the least, but not out of place in the Cornwall of those days, still in the horse and cart era and motor cars as uncommon as a white five pound note, which when presented was viewed with suspicion, especially in the rural areas. There was no doubt that when you crossed the Tamar from Devon, you entered another world, in speech, manners, food and general behaviour. Since the Cornish lacked humour, repartee always fell on stony ground. They seemed to be stuck in their insularity, and what lay beyond the Tamar was to them incomprehensible.

In 1935 the whole countryside was steeped in mythology, mostly related to weather lore; when to plant your spuds - the moon and tide and which quarter of the wind all being relevant, and superstition as to your behaviours on the Sabbath was paramount. I recall also a long chat with an old dear who ran a village post office, to the extent of selling a dozen stamps in a week. I happened to have cut my hand and bound my handkerchief round my thumb. This the good lady noticed, and in all seriousness tried to prevail upon me to allow her to demonstrate by the 'laying on of hands' how this gift she had, or said she had, could be transmitted to me, and thus I could avail myself of a healing power to practise, as she said, on 'my rich friends up-country.'

Another aspect of Cornish life both Audrey and I noticed and spoke of at the time was the almost complete lack of gardening appreciation. I am not talking about such gardens as Trewithen, Tregothnan, Trengwainton, Pencarrow, and the other famous ones, but Mr. and Mrs. Everyman's garden. They just did not exist and we searched for them time and again in the rural areas. We looked over stone walls into the front gardens, and found nothing except grass and weeds. The only garden I can recall with any flowers was one in front of a farmhouse, on the way round the Lizard, near Lanarth, where I saw for the first time Olearia semi-dentata, with its lilac aster-like flowers and its grey leaves, which the mildness of Cornwall will allow to grow, just as on the Chatham Islands, east of New Zealand. Remember that this was our first visit to Cornwall. We had heard all about the equable temperature and the famous garden at Tresco, and naturally expected to find gardens full of flowers. Instead there was a drabness, an utter ignorance of the possibilities the climate had given them. The ignorance was, I regret to say, due in part to the extreme poverty of the county. What spare money they had went on food. Even the farmhouse would have young calves in the grass patch in front of the house, and all along the country roads we saw cows tethered, and goats. On the credit side, one virtue the Cornish did have was the universal desire to help the visitor, and they would put themselves out to get whatever it was that you wanted. We once ran out of petrol on the Lizard, and went to a garage at Ruan Minor, only to find after a long walk that they had no petrol to sell. The chap in the garage rang up another called Zoar and found he had some, so he took me there and brought me back with a gallon in a can to where my car was stranded, refusing any monetary reward for his kindness.

Nothing was too much trouble for those Cornish people.

I returned from our holiday to the discipline of University life, knowing that it would be several weeks before I could see Audrey again. It was not in my nature to have spare time to sit twiddling my thumbs, so at the first opportunity I joined the Officers' Training Corps at the University. It was run by that famous Scots regiment, the Black Watch, with its long reputation for bravery in action, and it had an aura of glamour that attracted me. I had not given up my idea completely of going into the R.A.F., but here was a chance to serve my country, should the need arise, and I seized it with enthusiasm.

I began to discover that what looks superficially attractive is rarely so, upon close inspection. It was at one of the summer camps at Blair Atholl, beautifully situated alongside the River Dee in Perthshire, that I first experienced the working of the military mind. The Commander-in-Chief Scottish Command, was due to inspect us, and in the time-honoured way, 'spit-and-polish' was the order of the day. Boots were shined, equipment blancoed. Never was the old military adage - 'if it moves, salute it, if it doesn't, paint it' - more appropriate.

My problem was simply stated. Having a very slim build and weighing only around eight and a half stone, I had hips to match. They might have suited my athleticism, but in no way did they help toward keeping up a heavy kilt. The thing would simply not stay up as was intended. At the point of despair, an obvious solution suggested itself. I would arrange to be in the rear rank, furthest from the saluting base. That should save the embarrassment of being seen with a kilt dangling below the knee.

It probably would have escaped notice, but for the intervention of an especially thick sergeant-major. On the morning of the parade, with the troops drawn up on three sides of a square (the saluting base forming the fourth side), this individual decided to bring the rear rank to the fore, and vice-versa. So there I was, in the front row, with kilt well below the regulation line, facing the platform, now occupied by the Regimental Sergeant-Major who was casting his eye over the assembly prior to the entrance of the Big White Chief. He drew us all smartly to attention,then left the stand to march across the parade ground and stand directly in front of me.

"What's your name?" he demanded.

"Witherwick, Sergeant-Major."

"Your kilt is fully an inch below your knee, Witherwick. Get it up."

"It won't stay up," I answered.

He grabbed hold of the offending item and yanked it and me so hard I nearly lost balance. Standing back to observe the result, he saw the kilt promptly fall down. He came forward again, putting his knee in my stomach, and gave another mighty pull. The kilt came up, hovered for a moment and fell down. This time his patience was exhausted. He rushed at me, grabbed me by the scruff of the neck, hurled me into the back row and pulled the other man forward into the place I had vacated. Then he shouted to me. "For God's sake stay there with your bloody skirt!"

If I could have dug a hole in the parade ground and crawled into it, I would gladly have done so. Now everybody would know exactly who I was - the Black Watch OTC chap with the skirt!

Matters did not improve after that. Incessant rain turned the meadow around our camp into a quagmire on which our tents, duckboards and camp beds floated. It was a subdued and sodden detachment of would-be soldiers that struck camp and made its way back to Edinburgh.

Meanwhile, the time had come to put the theory of dentistry into practice. My first live patient was handed to me by Surgeon Alfred Mackay one Monday morning in March 1936 in the junior operating room of the hospital at the top of Chambers Street, Edinburgh, with the instruction "This patient requires conservation treatment to his lower left first premolar, this morning....." he glanced at the list to find my name, "Ah, Witherwick," he finished.

I always felt that the hesitant way in which Alf Mackay introduced me sowed the seeds of doubt in the mind of the sceptical, middle-aged Scot. He had no sooner sat down in the dental chair than he said, "Am I your first patient, my boy? I doubt you can do as good a job as this one." He pointed at a tooth. "I had it filled here twelve years ago."

It was not an encouraging start, but worse was to follow. I messed about with the preparation of the tooth, first giving him an injection, only to be told it was not necessary as the tooth did not hurt him. After being very careful not to get into the pulp[1], I was more thansurprised to find the decay I was removing was in fact coming out of the pulp chamber. At least I thought my injection was O.K., otherwise he would have hit the ceiling. But what to do next? My friend and companion in the Marchmont digs, J.P. McConville, was upstairs in the senior conservation room, and to him I went for help.

---

[1] The pulp is in the middle of the crown of the tooth, the point where all the main nerves, blood vessels and lymphatic canals meet : the engine room of the tooth.

Mac was introduced as a surgeon and proceeded to investigate my problem. After a bit of well-directed work, he announced to the patient that everything was fine, but the root canal would have to be filled first. It would need to be cleansed of dead material. At the mention of "dead" my patient became alert, and waxed lyrical about having been given an injection. What we had was a pathological exposure of the pulp, it having been killed by the quickly advancing decay.

Once again my lack of knowledge was being exposed. Mac very kindly did a bit of reaming[2] out of the root canal and left, saying I would be able to finish the filling. It always looks easy when someone else is doing it, but it never is when you come to do it yourself. After about ten minutes I suddenly found my root reamer meeting no resistance, and when removed from the tooth was covered in blood, and my patient in a great to-do, with a sudden stab of pain! Not knowing what had happened but assuming I had pushed the reamer through the apex of the root and into the bone and its blood vessels, I blandly stated to the none-too-pleased patient that I had finished cleaning out the root and would go and fetch Surgeon McConville for his examination. When I went upstairs and whispered to Mac about the blood, etc., he was soon back down to my patient, only to find the root canal now full of blood, and this supposedly a dead tooth! After many paper points to mop up the blood, Mac stopped his investigation and whispered. "You've put the reamer out through the side of the root, so you can't root-fill it now. Best thing to do is to get the tooth extracted!"

We withdrew and had a heated conference on the staircase outside. One thing was certain. Neither Alf Mackay nor any other house surgeon must find out about this appalling mess. Suddenly Mac had a brainwave and his face lit up. "Betty Dykes!" he said, as though pronouncing magic.

Betty was an understanding female student, known to us both, who was in the local anaesthetic department for her second and final period of instruction. We rushed into the students' common room, and there she was drinking coffee, laying the law down and smoking. The details of my sorry plight were revealed and she, good as gold, acquiesced in Mac's plan of action. The patient was taken down to the local anaesthetic department and handed into Betty's care. She knew how to make it right with Freddie Duval, the surgeon in charge, and

---

2 A reamer is an instrument used to remove organic debris in the root canal of a tooth, prior to doing a root filling.

extract the tooth.

Our plan worked, except that Betty, in her haste to get the offending tooth out before Duval had time to think, broke the crown off, and so had to get him to extract the root, fortunately not remarking on its imperfections! Meanwhile I was fretting downstairs, hovering between the main entrance and the local anaesthetic department, when, coming out of the Registrar's office, I almost knocked down my patient on his way out of the hospital. To my amazement he advanced towards me with outstretched hand, "I'm so glad to be rid of that tooth," he enthused. "It's given me Hell. I never wanted it filled, any road. Thank you my boy. I wish you luck in your career."

I was flabbergasted with all this, having in no measure deserved praise to my own mind. However, I pulled myself together and rushed to the swing door to open it for him in almost tearful gratitude.

In the hospital common room, Betty Dykes became a celebrity, and the story lost nothing by repeated telling. For me, it was the source of many a bad dream in the months to come.

As a student my sporting pastimes were not to be found in the billiard halls or the cinemas but rather in the open air, in the summer mainly on the golf course and in the winter on the football field. However, one incident, which I shall never forget, took place in the icy water of The Firth of Forth. Taking part in a Saturday afternoon sailing race our boat, when rounding the furthermost buoy, fell into the sea and Jack Ashton and myself were left clinging onto this buoy in the cold month of March, with an equally cold wind and water like ice. In all honesty, waiting to be rescued, after several hours was almost my eclipse and but for Jack's unselfish and manly support, this account would not now be written. That numbing cold still lingers even to-day in my mind's eye.

Somewhere about 1937, going down to Princes Street one evening for a drink, I ran into an old school friend up from Yorkshire in order to participate in the British Open Golf Championship. At the end of the evening's session I found myself cajoled into partnering him next morning for the start of the 'Open' at Muirfield. As far as I can recall one simply waited one's turn at the first tee, giving one's name and Club, in my case 'unattached', and paid, I believe, 5/-d and off we went. It was not our day, everything was either bunkered or out of bounds or just missed due, perhaps, to a happy go lucky frame of mind, resulting in our withdrawal from any further participation after the first round.

Chapter 4

HONEYMOON, 1937 - SCOTLAND

After that first encounter with a real patient, I was determined not to make such mistakes again. With the thorough training, that involved our attending regular surgeries at the hospital, we were able to build up our expertise. After all, it is only repeated practice that makes for a competent craftsman, given basic ability and sound knowledge of the fundamentals. So it was that I came to my final year with the full expectation of passing the final exams. I had written my thesis "What I Expect of Dental Practice" and sent it to The Dental Delineator, published by S.S. White, an American dental company, and had hopes of its eventual publication.

Before this, I was faced with a decision in my personal life. Audrey Williams and I saw very little of each other, due to being at opposite ends of the country. We had to save hard even to afford the fares to get together in vacations. It was an unsatisfactory situation, and there were temptations at University for a single man. In my case, this took the attractive female form of Violet Anderson, a Scots dental student from Kirkcaldy. She was good company, we had much in common, and we were becoming almost too intimate.

I knew that I could not go on seeing her and thinking about Audrey. My favourite game has always been cricket, and I felt that the situation I was getting into was not fair to Audrey - not "cricket." Accordingly I wrote to her in Cardiff, proposing that she got herself up to Edinburgh about the 7th of August for the purpose of marrying me! And she agreed.

The students were away on summer vacation and my good friend John McConville had gone home, leaving his single room in my digs vacant. Our landlady, Mrs. Woods, was very understanding, and fell in with my plans to use the room. My parents had been informed that I was going to Inverness to stay with Johnnie Proven, a close dental colleague, and I had fixed Alan Thomas, about to take his finals and already married, to bring his wife so that they could act as witnesses to my marriage with Audrey. I chose a Registry Office just round the corner from the Edinburgh Dental Hospital.

The deed was done. Audrey and I were man and wife after some six years of "walking out", and I so far not having earned a penny - hence the secrecy. Nobody was told, except Alan and his wife, who witnessed the ceremony and who appear on our Marriage Lines. Audrey and I could now live together as man and wife which we had not done before, so this honeymoon was going to be exciting.

Within an hour of the ceremony we set off in a 1925 Wolseley Hornet, which I had hired from, I think, Jimmy Trainer, now the Laird of Kelso, a worthy figure in the Scottish Border Country with his wife Marjorie, just as well qualified as Jummy himself. One day I hope to meet up with them again for a "crack". This honeymoon was certainly being done on a shoestring, as neither of us had any money, except what we had managed to extract from our parents to cover the so-called "holiday". I had even borrowed the tent.

Our first night was spent pitched in the bracken in the wilds of Glencoe. I remember it well. Innocents that we were, we had arrived at the height of the famous Glencoe mosquito season with no mosquito netting for our tent. Believe me, these insects meant business and no quarter given. We had a hell of a night, far removed from nuptial bliss, and as soon as dawn broke we packed up and were on our way to Inverness, where appropriate postcards were posted to our respective parents.

We then, having had a square meal somewhere, retraced our steps to Loch Ness to take the road to the Isles, a road I'd always wanted to travel, as the song, sung with such Scottish fervour, always stirs my heartstrings. It was my great great maternal grandfather who was a Macinder, a small chip of a Scottish clan under the umbrella of a large one. A one time farmer, he lost a leg in a wager race against the local squire at Spilsby, Lincs., he and his gig finishing in the ditch. He then took up the craft of clock-making, and I have one of his grandfather clocks to strike the hours and tell me the date here at Trelean, handed down as an heirloom.

It was on the road to the Isles that we came to that haunting

45

monument to Bonnie Prince Charlie at Glenfinnan. There was a rough area staked out as a car park, and the siting of this column to mark the Jacobite rebellion at the head of Loch Shiel is in keeping with a lost cause. We pushed on for Mannaig, the road very narrow, and after Glenfinnan, full of potholes, so that our progress was barely more than thirty miles per hour. At Loch Eilt, where we had planned to set our tent, the rain came down as if to wash us into the Loch itself, and of such persistent intensity that we would have been mad to think of setting up the tent.

About 2.30 a.m., we had had enough of the West Coast and retraced our steps. But something had happened to the headlights so that only the side-lights worked, with just enough glimmer to show where the road was. However, due to the potholes, the intense darkness and rain, our speed barely exceeded fifteen miles an hour, though with no traffic to contend with. Suddenly I became aware of two points of green light ahead, seemingly in the middle of this seven foot wide road, standing about eight feet high and set close together. What on earth could have such bright green lights, which as we got nearer seemed no more than nine inches apart, and had grown to the size of saucers? Here we were, in the middle of the Scottish Highlands on an unlit road little better than a cart-track, with lights too feeble to illuminate the strange thing blocking the road ahead. And this was supposed to be our honeymoon!

Worse was to follow. When I stopped and turned off the engine, we became aware of a stamping noise and what sounded like a steam engine coming towards us! My torch! - fortunately under the driving seat. With the window down I leant out and flashed it to see a massive stag, only some ten yards from the car, with steam coming out of its nostrils.

Holding the flashlight beam against the beast's eyes seemed to stimulate its aggressive behaviour. It kept coming on, lowering and raising its massive horns, standing all of eight feet high with a long, shaggy coat. I told Audrey to get down on the floor below the dashboard as I felt sure it was going to charge us, but when it was no more than three yards from the car I suddenly started to flick the flashlight beam across its face. This change of tactic appeared to register, as it stopped in its tracks, gave a massive snort, turned smartly to its left and just disappeared into the night.

It took us some time to recover from this encounter with a true "Monarch of the Glen," as magnificent a beast as any dedicated deerstalker could have wished to see. Our journey through the rain continued without further incident.

We spent the next few days doing short runs within easy reach of Inverness, so that postcards could continue to be sent back home. One trip was down Glen Urquhart to view the beautiful Glen Affric and Loch Affric. Another took us to Nairn, where we stayed a night near the golf course in a farmer's field, and I helped him for many hours to stook his corn, as he was using a horse and reaper. I think he thought I was a Scot, as I was wearing my Black Watch kilt, which I found most useful, not only as trews but as a rug on our sleeping bag at night.

It rained all that night and blew half a gale, so we never heard the other car come into the field, nor its passengers pitching their tent near to ours. The sight that met my eyes in the morning when I took a peep out of our tied tent flap was not merely surprising but hardly believable. In this pouring rain was a woman, squatting in front of their tent, holding a frying pan over a Primus stove. Standing over her was a man, fully dressed with a city-style overcoat complete with bowler hat, holding an umbrella over her while she fried his breakfast. I attracted Audrey's attention, and together we stared in wonderment at the scene.

After a trip to Beauly and its Firth, and carefully covering our tracks by arranging with another dental student colleague who lived in Inverness, - John Nixon I think his name was, - to post some cards we had written, it was my intention to round off the honeymoon by getting up to Wick. This was about 100 miles north from Inverness, and my reason was mainly egotistical as everyone called me "Wick" at Edinburgh. We set off early as I hoped to get to Wick by mid afternoon, and we did the first seventy miles in fine style. The road from Dingwall onwards had recently been resurfaced and there was hardly any traffic, even in mid August. Today I understand you can hardly get anywhere in Scotland during August without the frustrating delays caused by traffic jams.

At Helmsdale we found the road-construction gang and were told by them that the surface from there to Wick was in a pretty bad state. We soon found the truth of this, and no mistake. It was even worse than the road to the Isles. It was impossible to miss all the potholes, some of them cavernous. The inevitable happened, and into one of these we went. The right front wheel dropped alarmingly and we stopped!

Investigation showed that all the leaves in one half of the main front spring had broken. The other half was held by no more than half an inch in the middle clamp box. What to do about it was a tricky problem. To get it repaired we would have to go back to Inverness, some 80 miles. Certainly this road was very good, whereas we were only some thirty-five miles from Wick, over a terrible road. Once this good piece of spring held by half an inch of clamp failed, that would be the finish and we would have to sit waiting for help. Nonetheless, we decided to risk taking the shorter route, and set off with our hearts in our mouths, rarely out of bottom gear at no more that 10 m.p.h., trying to circumnavigate these awful holes in the road. We finally made Wick at 6.15 p.m. and drove straight to the only garage in the place according to my A.A. book - Robertson's Garage. It was still open, and Mr. Robertson was sitting on a stool in his cubby hole of an office doing his day's book-keeping. He looked up at me and said, "What's the trouble?"

I told him and forthwith he accompanied me outside to inspect the Hornet. He checked the spring, then opened the bonnet and took the engine number.

"Will you pay for a telephone call to Inverness?" he enquired.

"Why, yes," I said, so back to the cubby hole he went to put in a call to the supply garage at Inverness, giving them the details. Yes, they had such a spring.

Mr. Robertson then turned to me, "Will you pay for it to be sent up tomorrow by plane?"

"Yes," I said.

Back he went to the phone to recheck that it was the correct spring, which would be put on the 8.30 a.m. plane. Down went the receiver of the phone and he turned to me, "Provided it gets here alright, I will have your car ready at 12.00 midday tomorrow!"

And it was, just as he promised. I don't think there is any garage in England today to give service like that off the cuff.

The only other thing I remember about Wick was sitting outside the tent and reading the Daily Telegraph at 12.15 a.m. by daylight.

Next day, having first bought a Daily Express in Wick, we set off for John o' Groats. We drove straight up to the front door of the hotel, at about 12.30 p.m. There was not another car outside and nobody in the bar except mine host, and here we were in the middle of August 1938.

I had noticed the banner headlines in the Daily Express I had bought in Wick, and after chatting to our host over drinks, I said to him, "Have you seen the papers today?"

"Why, no," he said, "ours don't get here until about 1.30. Anything special?"

"I should say so. You're banner headlines in the Daily Express."

"What the hell for?" he demanded.

"I'll go to the car and get the Express."

The headline went something like this:

TAXI WATERLOO - JOHN O' GROATS!

What had happened was a party of Americans had got off the Boat Train into Waterloo Station from Southampton and then went straight to the taxi rank and asked one of the drivers if he would take them and their luggage straight to John o' Groats. Apparently they were already on their way.

Mine host was much amused. "Well, I hope they make it," he said. "We could do with a bit of publicity. Things are a bit slack, as you can see!"

I told him about our misfortune with our car on the awful road. "Yes," he agreed, "it's one of the reasons so few people come up here from Inverness. The sooner this road is finished the better for us here."

Whilst we were having our second round of drinks I walked over to the window overlooking the road and the car park, and there to my amazement, just driving in, was a typical London taxi, with the top full of luggage. "Look, here come those Yanks in the taxi!" I shouted.

Our man rushed to the window. "Well, I'll be buggered!" he exclaimed, as though he had just witnessed a miracle.

Audrey and I decided we would get away and not be involved with all the socialising that was bound to follow. I noticed as I passed the taxi on the way to our car that there were six in this party of Americans - one in the front with the driver, three on the back seat and the other two on the drop seats behind the driver's seat. The vehicle was grossly overloaded, but I had no doubt that the traditional generosity of Americans and the shrewd nature of London cab-drivers combined to make it a worthwhile trip for all concerned.

In the bar I had found out that John o' Groats was not the furthest point north in the British Isles. Dunnet Head, some dozen miles along the coast, was two miles further out. After going to the jetty and seeing some fishermen unloading lobsters from a cage kept underwater beneath the jetty in the Pentland Firth (I still have a photograph with Audrey to recall the scene), we set off for Dunnet Head. To reach it you have to leave the main road which goes on to Thurso and take to minor roads, travelling alongside a small loch. I noticed a large hawk hovering over the loch. Pointing it out to Audrey I said, "I think that's a Golden Eagle," though I had never seen one before.

Soon afterwards the road dipped down and came near to the sea, then descended to a little cove, wherein sat a lovely, tiny harbour with carefully stacked boulders to form its walls. It all looked so attractive, with a farmhouse sitting at the top of the small field which bordered the harbour, that we stopped the car and just sat absorbing the beauty of it all. Enthralled by this little harbour and its utilitarian beauty, we decided to approach the farm to see if we could stay and pitch our tent. A nice, youngish farmer called Macintosh greeted us and made us feel welcome. He went out of his way to make us as comfortable as possible, including asking us into the farm kitchen at night for a chat and warm-up before retiring to our little tent set in the fields overlooking this fairylike harbour.

I found out from our farmer friend that the harbour did in fact belong to him. It was all part and parcel of the farm. He thought that it was probably the only privately owned harbour in Scotland, and it had been paid for by the Earl of Caithness, who many years ago saw the need for such a small safe harbour. There was no other means for the farmers of Caithness to sell their produce, given the poor condition of the roads and the distances to a place of sale, whereas a small sailing ship in, say, mid-September could safely sail from Leith, Edinburgh, and tie up in this small harbour whilst the corn was manually loaded. The Earl had also built the barn standing near the road, where the corn could be stored whilst awaiting shipment, and the castle we had noticed some distance back. This enjoyed magnificent views out over the Pentland Firth to the Old Man of Hoy and to the three hundred foot high cliffs of Dunnet Head, rising sheer out of the sea, and the home of thousands of sea birds. Well, this castle was the Castle of Mey, the seat of the Earl, and the Loch which the hawk was quartering was the Loch of Mey, and yes, it was a Golden Eagle.

Furthermore, my friend informed me, he tried to have a swim in the harbour each day throughout the year, when the sea was up into the harbour; also, the massive kitchen fireplace was home to a peat fire, which had never gone out for over forty years. We paid our respects to this glowing fire on several occasions. The more I looked

50

at this little harbour the more I appreciated the sheer hard manual work involved by men and horses, to get the massive blocks of stone from some nearby quarry over muddy roads, and then to fight the tide. They had to be set so neatly and securely, one upon the other, to withstand the battering of the seas coming straight at them from the Pentland Firth, a sea to shake the timbers of both ships and men, especially those from Scrabster in their lifeboat, a wee village just up past Dunnet Head and Thurso.

In consequence I took photos of this harbour from all angles with my box camera, little realising that forty-five years on, I would present one of these photos, enlarged and framed, to the Queen Mother.

Within two days of pitching our tent by this harbour, which I believe was called Ham Harbour, we were asked if we would like to go with our farmer friend to Thurso market. We were a bit surprised on getting into the car, however, to find that we had to keep an eye on three sheep and a collie dog in the back! We had not gone above ten miles when we found ourselves passing along the shoreline of a lovely open shelving beach with big rolling waves coming up the golden sands. My wife and I almost simultaneously exclaimed, "What a lovely beach for surf-riding."

After attending the market at Thurso and seeing his sheep sold, we retired to the Market Inn for lunch, and it was during this repast that our friend dragged out of us all about surf-riding, a sport apparently not known about in those parts. As an ardent swimmer he persisted in his questions so much that after lunch he marched us off to a carpenter's shop in Thurso where we described the type of surf-boards needed and the carpenter, there and then, set to work in order to have two ready by four o'clock.

In the meantime our friend took us to look at Scrabster, nestling by the Pentland Firth, where the liefeboat was kept. The outcome of all this was that we, Audrey and I, undertook to give a demonstration of surf-riding on Dunnet Bay beach, at 5.00 p.m. the following day, when the tide would be right. We were somewhat surprised to find on arrival that about ten people had turned up to witness this new-fangled swimming sport. We both ran down to the sea, surf-boards at the ready and dashed into the foaming water, only to get just about the biggest shock of our lives. The water was as cold as ice, but with all those people watching we just had to go through with it, which we did, and gave a fairly good demonstration with some good runs. After

51

fifteen minutes I could stand the cold no longer and came out. My teeth were chattering to such an extent I could hardly articulate my words and took off to run up and down the beach, but even this strenuous exercise failed to get my circulation back to normal.

To my discomfort and to a lesser degree my wife's, someone from those gathered on the shoreline suggested we all get into the cars and go to a cottage where we could have a game of tennis and get some hot drinks. The cottage we arrived at was akin to a 'But and Ben' type, and in front of it was a bit of tufty grass which was being slowly consumed by a tethered cow. So this was the tennis court! A bit similar to village cricket pitches I've played on around Scarborough, where the first step was a spade to shift the cow pats, and this is what took place in Caithness within sound of the Pentland waves.

Then two broom handles were knocked in and a bit of fishing net stretched across. The rackets were really museum pieces, consisting of fishing net stretched across a bent willow branch, with other pieces of wood tied and bound to make a thick handle and thus, after some difference of opinion as to where the one tennis ball was likely to be found, play commenced. It certainly did warm one up with the effort of trying to run on this tufty grass, and to get the ball over the net it had to be walloped with one hell of a clout, as the net on the racket was devoid of any pretence of tension.

We were then called inside and hot drinks handed round, most folk sitting on the floor near another lovely peat fire with its special aroma which is like no other. Peat is the staple fuel of country folk in Caithness, where there are hardly any trees. Stone walls of large slabs standing on end enclose the small fields. Apparently they don't get much snow up in the far north of the county, as the wind is usually too strong for it to fall and lie. What hospitable folk they are up here in the far north, where English is so well spoken and with a clarity so different from Glasgow, and in general the south of Scotland. It is as different as the East Riding of Yorkshire is to the West Riding.

We left Caithness in pouring rain after delaying our departure hoping it would cease. But we had to drive through a steady downpour, and after about nine hours of almost continuous driving I had to pull off the road near Pitlochry to save myself from going to sleep. Awakened by the dawn, we found we had parked ourselves in the drive of somebody's house for our few hours of sleep. We arrived back in Edinburgh early on the Monday morning, the end of our secret honeymoon, Audrey to go straight back to Cardiff and I to continue my dental studies in Edinburgh. Our married life had come to a sudden end and we had to thank Hitler for giving us the opportunity to get married again the following year, but this time "officially", and to enable us to be together as man and wife once more. Oh yes! But it was Hitler and my conscience and sense of responsibility that kept us from having children. I had volunteered for the R.A.F. and fully expected overseas service, and war is war. One never knows the dangers and hardships a young mother with child can encounter.

When in Caithness we both acknowledged the similarity to Cornwall, the high velocity wind and lack of trees, stone hedges, slabs of stone set on edge and plenty of desolate area seemingly devoid of man, beast or bird, and the sea. However, the chill of winter by the Pentland Firth is a very different kettle of fish to the equitable climate of Cornwall, and so is the hardy character of the people who live there.

It is often said how small the world is and so it can be when you meet up with lost firiends in unexpected places. So it can be with incidents. Who could have foreseen my box camera photo of that lovely little harbour sitting below the Castle of May could be my gift to the Queen Mother 38 years on in 1983 when she opened the Duchy Hospital, Truro? The Queen Mother could hardly believe her eyes to see this little harbour handed to her in Cornwall. When the Queen Mother found the photo had been taken on my honeymoon the conversation became near motherly understanding. Everything comes to those who wait, provided you live long enough. If you follow this line of thought to its logical conclusion you could hope to meet up with the Archangel Gabriel and his hounds.

Chapter 5

CRISIS - L.D.V. - THE BLITZ

It was not easy to concentrate on my studies after the eventful honeymoon, and the time for taking my finals was fast approaching. I was fairly confident about the outcome, encouraged by the practical experience of attending patients at the Edinburgh Dental Hospital. One day after evening practice here, I stopped on the way back to my digs for a drink at an old public house known as "The 'ole in the Wa'." It was just round the corner from the Hospital and almost opposite that lovely monument to a dog called "Bobbie,"........ who when his master died and was buried in the Church of the Grass Market, went and sat by the grave day after day and would not leave his vigil. Folk brought food to him there, and so he lived for many years, never to leave that grave. When he died, a monument to his faithful memory was erected, and there it stands to this day.

I often went to the public house for a drink after evening practice or for my lunch - a pie and another half-pint, eightpence all told. Well, one of the locals had had his eye on me apparently, and that night had finally faced up to unburdening his soul and the state of his mouth to me. After getting the gist of what he was after, I suggested we removed ourselves from the bar into the ill-lit back room, where sometimes we played darts. When I examined his mouth and teeth, the stench was almost more that I could stand. Suddenly he began to cry and blurted out that he had not the courage to go into hospital to have his teeth out. Would I please take them out there and then for him?

His agony of mind and this heartfelt appeal forced me to do what I could in a most unhygienic way. As soon as I said I would, he whipped out a half bottle of whisky and drank half of it! I waited a few minutes for this hard stuff to circulate, then sat him down on one of the rickety chairs and proceeded to pull out all his remaining rotten loose teeth with my fingers. He never made a murmur; just sat with his mouth open, tears streaming down his face. When it was all done, he washed his mouth out with more neat whisky and produced another large bottle from a newspaper-wrapped parcel under his chair and gave it to me. I returned it, shook his hand, and left the pub, somewhat emotional myself.

Now exams were upon me. They were more comprehensive than is common today, consisting of two main parts; medicine and surgery in relation to dentistry, and dentistry itself. Effectively this meant two days of written papers, one of orals, and two of practical operations. If you passed the medical part and not the dental, then the part you had passed did not require you to sit that again. To my amazement, the results showed that while I had passed the medical, I failed the dental exam in one small area - dental metallurgy - and because of this, had to sit the entire dental final again, not just the metallurgy part but even worse it would be six months before I could re-sit the exam. The agony and injustice of it ate into my soul, not least the fatuous question put to me by the examiner in the oral. "Tell me, Mr. Witherwick, the main differences between the manufacture of pig iron and wrought iron." I could not see the relevance of it, didn't know the difference and said so. What if I failed again? The nightmare of reality drove my mind to fever pitch and utter instability. For three days and nights I paced the streets of Edinburgh, eating just to live and sleeping where pure weariness forced me to. The culmination of this mental agony and sheer physical exhaustion was, by the third night, a resolution, nay, a resolve, to finish myself. The very thought of my father, now having to keep me for a further six months or even more, and little Audrey, awaiting news in far Cardiff, my secret wife, was devastating, so to the "Bridges" my courage took me. Oh yes, to commit suicide needs spirit, not cowardice, since I had done no wrong, just a failure. So at about 1.00 a.m., alone, standing on the parapet of the "Bridges" holding on to a dimly lit lamp standard, on the verge of jumping to death, a voice from out of the darkness - "Oi, there!"

I was so startled I swung around the lamp post and jumped down to the pavement to run along towards the North British Hotel, then along Princes Street all the way to the "Mound" and half way up there I could run no further, collapsed onto the pavement, crying from exhaustion and what? - sheer relief that I was still alive I suppose.

Whatever else, the episode gave me strength and a new resolve to carry on. I would go and see the Dean of the Faculty, Dr. Hutchinson, whom I found next morning closeted with the Vice Dean, Col. Findlayson, to seek his advice. However, his response was far from encouraging. "I feel you should have known the answer to that particular question" the Dean told me. "Possibly if you had spent a little more time with your studies and a little less in organising the appeal to fund a new wing for the Dental Hospital, you might not have found yourself in this difficulty."

I was taken aback by this unnecessarily spiteful remark and was delighted when Col. Findlayson sprang to my defence.

"Witherwick was giving his time and energy voluntarily to help the Hospital," he said. "As to the metallurgy question, I consider it was by no means a proper one." He turned to me. "Now Witherwick, I suggest you go home until Christmas, swot up there, and return in the New Year. Then we'll see if we can find you a house surgeon's job until March when you sit your Dental Finals again. I'm sure you'll get through next time."

There was nothing for it but to take his advice and return to Hull.

My father took the news philosophically. He knew that I had done my best and did not blame me for failing to answer the strange question on pig iron, whose relevance I have still to understand.

Being at home was quite different now and I missed mother. She died the previous year, succumbing to pneumonia, a disease that killed thousands of people annually before the advent of anti-biotics. Today a course of penicillin would probably have spared her for a long and useful life. The atmosphere of the house had changed, and with my school-friends mostly working full-time or away, life was rather dull.

At least I was able to study, and on my return to Edinburgh in January 1939, took up the house-surgeon's job. This proved to be my salvation. The job really lifted me, and having to find answers to the many questions I was asked by the junior students, I knew far more that I had done at my first examination. At the second attempt, I passed with high marks. I was now a fully-fledged Dental Surgeon, straining at the leash to get out into the world and earn some money at last.

One would have thought that it would be easy to find a practice after all the years of training. But here we were in the middle of the Depression and with mass unemployment - conditions I had been sheltered from during my studies. And in the very month I sat my second finals, Germany's annexation of Czechoslavakia recalled the spectre of war. Of more immediate importance, I was at odds with my father. He was well known and respected in Hull, and proposed using his influence to secure for me a good position in the city. It was obvious to him that everything favoured that view. Better the devil you know..... In London I would be on my own professionally, not knowing a soul. From his experience and what he had heard, it would be hard to earn a living in dentistry with the cut-throat competition and all the bustle and hassle.

My contrary view was that I wanted to gain practical experience as an assistant before launching out on my own. Moreover, too many people in Hull knew me as a boy, and I felt would not take me seriously as a Dental Surgeon. Finally, having a practice on my father's back did not measure up to making my name as a dentist from my own skill and endeavour.

There was to be no reconciling our points of view, and when I announced my decision, I could see he was very hurt. On the morning of my departure, he gave me £50 to tide me over, but did not come to see me off at Paragon station.

I really don't know how I had the courage to do it and defy my father's opinion. But worse was to come, a lot worse. Full of my own importance I booked in at a good Hotel off The Strand, Berners Hotel, largely because, when I first came to London in 1926 for the Wembley Exhibition with my parents, we stayed there.

There were four main dental houses in London in 1939, and I called on each in turn to see their Registrars in respect of a job. It was soon apparent that I was not the only one looking for a job, and usually there were about six or more hopeful applicants sitting on the bench outside the Registrar's office. We were called in the order of arrival, so I always seemed to have about two hours to wait. By the end of the week I had seen them all and got the same answer, "I will let you know as soon as anything comes along. At the moment there are very few dentisits needing assistants, and those that do, seem to wish to interview a London qualified man."

"London qualified." That bit always infuriated me, as though coming from Edinburgh implied a foreign degree.I noticed that all these other chaps looking for a job came from London hospitals, and nobody from the provinces at all, let alone Scotland. As a last hope I went to S.S. Whites, Great Portland Street, on the Friday afternoon of that dreadful week, to see if I could see the Managing Director. I had recently written an article for their magazine "The Delineator," published in their May issue, and my photograph was on the front of it. I did in fact see the Manager, and a cup of tea was brought in. I also met a Mr. Batstone, who was called in by the Manager, but it was the same story I had heard all the week. There was no job - at least, not for those from the provinces, and not many it seemed even for those with London qualifications. The streets of London were not paved with gold.

As the weeks went by with no work, I became more and more bitter. I could not see that Ramsay MacDonald, the then Labour Prime Minister, was doing anything for the unemployed, many of whom would have cried for joy if they could have had the chance to clean out the lavatories or sweep the streets. Here was I, with first-class qualifications, all at my working father's expense, unemployed and walking the streets of London, with no dole. It was hardly surprising that when at last my luck turned, and I was given the job of re-opening a closed dental practice, in Well Hall Road, Eltham, London S.E.9., I cried for joy - quite literally. It was a branch practice, the main one being in a more salubrious district. My surgery was within a working class estate, at the top of a hill, with the clanging of trams passing all day, right up to one o'clock in the morning. Audrey and I were quite unused to the noise, so we could never get off to sleep until after the last tram had gone by on its clanking way to the Woolwich Depot.

I was paid £3 a week, less 12/6 for rent, and my wife thrown in as nurse/receptionist/cook/cleaner and general skivvy. There was very little work to start with and what there was mostly came in after five o'clock, so we made appointments up to 8.30 p.m.

As I was just sitting doing nothing all day I went to see my boss and asked if I could seek some part-time work during the day, as my wife could hold the fort and make appointments for the evening.

The L.C.C. was advertising then for qualified dentists to undertake part-time work in the school clinics. I applied and went for an interview at County Hall. I was offered four sessions, that is equivalent to two days' work. So, within two months of going to London, not knowing a soul, I was earning six pounds ten shillings a week. In 1939 this was good money, and I had a roof over our heads for 12/6. I even thought of playing golf on a Saturday afternoon.

It was not long afterwards that the clouds of war started to gather in earnest. Parliament was re-called for an emergency sitting in mid-

August 1939, and Ernest Bevin the Labour spokesman castigated the Government led by Neville Chamberlain for re-arming, when, as he said, there was no apparent sign of Hitler renouncing his assertion to Chamberlain at Munich that he would not reclaim by force any more territory in Europe. Such was the view of the Labour Shadow Foreign Secretary. Within three weeks Hitler invaded Poland, and once again we were at war with Germany. Neville Chamberlain's piece of paper signed by Hitler had at least given the country a year to pull itself up by its boot straps.

I had offered my services to the R.A.F.V.R., and on the pretext of expecting to be called to the Colours, immediately organised our second wedding, this time in a Registry Office at Bradford, Yorks., four days after war was declared. Hitler had at least given us the opportunity to throw off the cloak of secrecy we had to maintain to our family in respect of our first marriage in Edinburgh a year earlier.

With Audrey now actively helping me, my dental affairs in London went forward by leaps and bounds. We became very busy at this practice I was building up, and the L.C.C. meantime advertised vacancies for permanent dental surgeon posts. I applied with the knowledge that they already knew what my work was like, and had every hope of being successful.

The interview at County Hall before the full Health Committee of this august Council soon dispelled any such optimism. I was only asked questions by the Chief Medical Officer, who went so far as to state that he had never seen such good references from an applicant before, and the Senior Dental officer mentioned that I was already working part-time for the Council. My work had proved highly satisfactory, and my organising abilities, as outlined by the Dean of the Faculty at Edinburgh University, would be much appreciated as they, the Dental Department of the L.C.C., were at present engaged on a major re-organisation scheme.

So far so good. Nobody else from the entire committee asked me any questions and I left the room thinking I could not have done better. Then they all cast their vote, most of them in open-necked shirts and boiler suits. I was not even on the short-list. It was hardly believable.

The reason for my rejection by this Labour controlled committee was given to me by the doorman in County Hall, and also by the Senior Dental Officer himself. I was wearing my public school tie so I was obviously one of "them" and not one of "us".

59

It was actually a blessing in disguise. Within a week of this rejection, I was invited to see the Senior Dental officer at County Hall, who asked me if I could undertake several more sessions a week. At the satisfactory end of this interview, as he showed me out of his office, he said, "I do hope you will apply again for a permanent post, but bear in mind it is not advisable to wear a red tie if there is a bull in the field!"

However, it was "once bitten twice shy". Never again would I get involved with socialism in my work, I resolved. It was as well I could not foresee the advent of the National Health Service.

It was only a few weeks after Dunkirk that I was faced with a major crisis. I was doing well in this practice at Eltham, so much so that I decided to see my boss and find out if he was prepared to sell me the practice. He procrastinated by getting his accountant to prepare a price, which, when it finally arrived, was so unrealistic that I lost my temper. I asked him how such a ridiculous figure had been arrived at, and it was his answer that made me blow my top.

"Well" he said, "if you go on as well as you are doing, my accountant thinks in a couple of years the practice will be worth this figure."

Unfortunately he lost his temper too, and there and then gave me a week's notice. If I was not out by then he would put the bailiffs in!

Well, to put it bluntly, we were in a hell of a fix. We had little or no money, and with the country under the threat of invasion, morale at its lowest ebb following Dunkirk, I decided that an appeal to his better nature was the only practical course. We were supposed to be professional colleagues, and to put me and my wife out on the streets within a week would not do him any good when the news was spread around. He relented and extended the notice to two weeks - big of him I must say! However, it did give me a bit more time to try and help myself. We did not just sit moaning about our predicament, and nobody was going to help us unless we helped ourselves.

They say that the Lord helps those that help themselves, and one day something interesting turned up. We rushed off to look at a house with a built-on annexe of a surgery, over at Chessington North, wherever that was! What I was not prepared for was the bloke himself who was trying to sell me the place. He was a medical man of the Jewish faith, and could he talk! I'm not too bad at that myself, but this fellow left me speechless. He had an answer to all my questions, even before I had opened my mouth!

We left full of hope. It was just what we needed to make a start to create my own practice from scratch. A nice new house, with the practice attached in a separate single-storey building alongside a corner site, garden front and back, on a new, clean estate with a row of six local shops, and only a couple of minutes' walk from the Northern Line Station.

But where could we get the money? Driving back home, all I could think of was to go and see the Bank Manager. And another minor problem, why was this Jewish doctor giving up such a wonderful site? It just did not add up. Did the drains smell? or had he discovered dry rot in the roof? It all seemed so unreal. Just what we wanted, handed to us on a plate, all except for the money to buy it.

The next morning I was round to my Bank, Martins, at Bexley, Kent. The Manager, whom I had not met before, was, to say the least, a wet blanket.

"We don't advance money, Mr. Witherwick, unless there is security. From what you have hold me, you have no security, except your bank account, which, at £115, is no security at all for this house and surgery annexe."

However, after pestering him he kindly gave me five addresses in the City of London where I might be able to raise the money, or some of it. I drove straight up to the City from Bexley and spent the rest of the day going to all these five big finance houses, but it was the same each time. They more or less laughed in my face. "You want to buy a house and start a non-existent practice when everyone is waiting for the bombs to drop, and the country next on the list for Hitler to invade? The best thing you can do, my boy, is to get into uniform!"

I returned home a very dejected person indeed. It was while I was eating my hurried snack before commencing evening surgery, that a flash of light appeared in my darkness.

I had played a few rounds of golf with a dental representative of S.S. White's Dental House, and he had mentioned that his wife's brother worked for a big London insurance company, and had advised me to contact this man if I ever wanted any insurance. That evening I got my golf friend on the phone and told him of my predicament. Within an hour I was talking to a Mr. A. Buckingham, representative of the Royal London Mutual Insurance Company, Finsbury Square, the upshot of which was that he would ventilate the matter in the morning when he got to his office. But he sounded hopeful in what he said, so I plucked up courage and phoned the Jewish doctor, determined to get a few answers to my questions.

The reason he was selling his house and practice was in fact that due to the outbreak of war the building company had now given up, and the rest of the estate would not be built. As this doctor had only recently started in practice, his future prospects of attracting patients had vanished like the early morning mist, since those already in residence were already on other doctors' lists. All this did not affect my commencing a dental practice, as dentists don't have lists, and patients can go where they like.

Good news soon came. The Royal London Mutual would arrange for a survey of the property, and in the light of this would advise me of the amount they would advance as a mortgage, having collateral security with an insurance policy on my life. Whilst this survey was going on I had another bit of urgent, and as it turned out, Jewish, business to conduct.

Contained within the back pages of my British Dental Journal was a 'For Sale' notice of complete surgery equipment, London, East End. By phone I was able to find out what it mainly consisted of, and with little or no messing about, agreed to buy the lot for fifty-seven pounds. My friend, our local chemist on Well Hall Road, agreed to come with me on his half day. I hired an open lorry and off we went. It turned out to be one of these shop-fronted practices in a rather seedy neighbourhood, and to my surprise, I found myself again dealing with a Jew. He was like a cat with two tails, and wasted no time in telling me why he was selling up - he had secured a permanent post with the L.C.C., and, from his point of view, a reserved secure post with no fear of conscription into the armed forces. he was over the moon. Yet here was I, buying his equipment to start a new practice, whilst marking time awaiting my call to the Colours, for which I had volunteered. It reminds me of the two men behind bars; one saw mud and the other saw the stars.

Everything went like a house on fire, once we had overcome the difficulty of getting the very heavy dental chair out and on to the lorry, aided by willing passers-by and a good deal of wit and good humour. We soon had the rest of the equipment on board, then this exuberant Jewish colleague said, "You can have the waiting room chairs, etc. Take the lot, and the workshop, and the office desk." All this in a back room. We even took the linoleum and light fittings, in fact stripped the place, all for fifty-seven quid! I think the man felt safe from Hitler under the powerful umbrella of the L.C.C. hence his generosity to me!

The insurance company survey resulted in my having to find £250. I rang my father, who was unable to help, at least not for some weeks. Next I rang my wife's father, who was not in a position to put such a sum on the table either. My last call was to Pearson Crabtree, my sister Enid's husband. yes, he could find £200 and would put it in the post. So we were nearly there, all but £50, though my own resources were by now reduced to just over £40.

I decided to phone the doctor, and this time he was going to listen to me if he wanted to sell his property. And he did! He reduced his price by £50, so we had secured a roof over our heads and the surgery annexe. We moved our bits and pieces of furniture and the surgery equipment in a hired van on the Saturday, the last day of the 14 days' notice my bad-tempered ex-colleague had given me before. That night, I remarked to Audrey, "everything is paid for and I've got £15 left."

The practice took off like a rocket, hardly giving us time to settle in. I even had a chap wanting a tooth out on the Monday morning, with the surgery in utter chaos and before I had even put my plate up! The good doctor had done a marvellous job in spreading the news of my arrival. Within a couple of months the evening surgery was going up to 9.30 p.m., and even during the blackout, and I was doing four days a week for the L.C.C. up in the City. But nearly everyone thought I was mad, as well as a B.F. for starting up on my own in the middle of a war, and I waiting for my call-up papers.

I remember one anaesthetist doctor in a London clinic saying, "Why, you could have a bomb drop and flatten the lot!"

My reply was oddly prophetic, as I said, "If any bombs come down they are more likely to hit Buckingham Palace than my semi-detached."

As it happened, I was coming from my clinic in Peckham Rye, having seen and heard the battle overhead, when a chap ran past me shouting, "They've 'it the Palace, the buggers!" at the top of his voice. News spread quickly in those hectic days.

When the war really hotted up we seemed to be right there with it, and I began to wonder what I had volunteered for.

Nearly every Sunday we set off into the Surrey countryside in the car for a bit of fresh air. This was in fact my first new car, the other cars I had owned being very much second-hand. It was a Morris Minor saloon, and cost £148 delivered to my house, with four gallons in the tank!

We happened to be in the hotel at Box Hill, near Leatherhead, having afternoon tea, on that special Sunday in September, when, on the six o'clock news, it was announced that our 'Spits' and Hurricanes had shot down over a hundred enemy fighters. All, or most of the day, we had been watching these dog-fights up in the clear blue sky, and seeing planes plummeting downwards with black smoke pouring from them.

Little did we realise on that lovely sunny day, that we were in fact watching the air battle that saved England from invasion, won by those courageous "few", many volunteers, who had spent their weekends at aero clubs up and down the country, together with the gallant Regulars of the Royal Air Force.

Anthony Eden, the Foreign Secretary, had already announced the formation of the Local Defence Volunteers, and I had enlisted the next morning, riding on my bike up to R.A.F. Chessington, which was then the Balloon Barrage H.Q. There were sixteen of us in our platoon, 3 Rifles and 4 Tin Hats, and we did all-night duty every fourth night at the Oxshot/Epsom/Leatherhead/Kingston Cross Roads, and used a small country cottage right in the corner of a field as our H.Q. - and the Fox & Hounds pub for refreshment until it shut down for 'time'.

It was whilst I was in the L.D.V. that I came nearest to actual warfare and danger. I was the only one with a car, and due to a terrible flash one night, which lit up the whole countryside, as well as a very loud bang or crack, we were convinced the Jerries had landed somewhere between us and Epsom. We set off to Epsom, fanning out across the fields, and met up with the Epsom crowd who also thought the same as we did. So, it was decided that somebody should get to Kingston Territorial H.Q. to report and sound the church bells. I offered to go, and ran back to get my car and set off as fast as I dared, driving with only blacked-out sid-lights. I made my report, but was prevented from ringing Kingston church bell until the Colonel T.A. i/c had received confirmation of my story from Epsom, which he was able to contact by an army telephone line. He was told the same story as mine, but no definite information of parachute landings. I was told to get back to my post.

Later, when the anti-aircraft set up a big battery at Hinchley Wood, we found ourselves in big trouble at our post on the crossroads, since we soon found from very near misses that the shell caps from this battery splattered all around us. Consequently, when the battery opened up, those of the platoon out on duty dived straight into the ditch.

We stopped all cars after midnight and demanded to see the identity cards. I stopped a big limousine one night and asked the front seat passenger for his card. This was not forthcoming, on some pretext or other. Since it was mandatory for everyone to carry the card, I kept on with my demands, whilst he kept telling his driver to drive on. He then said, "Don't you know who I am?"

When I said I did not, he said, "I'm Beaverbrook."

To which I replied, "Very good, Sir, but I still wish to see your identity card."

With this he put his hand inside his jacket, pulled out his wallet and produced his card and held it against my torch.

"Can I get to bed now?" he asked.

"Yes, Sir. Sorry," I said.

"No need to apologise, that's what you're here for. Goodnight and good luck." Off he went.

One Sunday morning, taking my wife to see my aunt and uncle, Winnie and Arthur Markham who lived off the North Circular Road, we were passing through Kingston on a grey and misty day, when the traffic lights changed from green to amber as we approached them in the town centre. At the same moment as we stopped on the red light, a two-engined Heinkel bomber swooped down from this low grey ceiling, and to our utter stupefaction, bore down on us with all guns firing. They were not far out, as the bullets were straddling the width of the road, just three yards in front of the car. It was an astonishing spectacle with people on the pavement just hurling themselves down flat and a poor woman with a pram throwing herself across it. As the lights changed to green, we drove off. Fortunately nobody was hit, and we, like law-abiding citizens, just sat in our car with the engine running, patiently waiting for the lights to change, so that we could move out of the war zone!

Certainly there was the lighter side to the battle of Britain. One night, sitting in my hot bath, there was a swish and a resounding thud, the whole house swayed to the blast, and within seconds I was sitting in a bath with barely two inches of water in it!

This bomb dropped only a hundred yards away and blasted two houses, with the crater on the pavement. Then again, one evening about 9.30 a patient had been driven by his aching tooth to leave the safety of the air raid shelter which was nearby and sought my help. As his pain was acute and caused by an abscess, it was necessary to give him a general anaesthetic in order to remove this infected tooth. I had just got him under and was on the verge of getting my forceps on to his tooth, when down came a bomb, rocking the surgery to its foundations. Everything on the shelves, instrument-trolley, and bottles of medicaments at the top of the cabinet just crashed onto the floor. I fell backwards, and very nearly hit my head on the edge of the wash basin, while the patient crumpled up on the foot-rest of the dental chair, still under the effects of the anaesthetic.

I had to wait for him to come round before he could be manoeuvred on to the seat of the dental chair again, as his weight was such that all my efforts to lift him proved useless. We had had another near miss, and after clearing up the worst of the shambles, we both had a cigarette. As his tooth was still giving him excruciating stabs of pain, I reluctantly administered another general anaesthetic, and this time got the tooth out.

Giving a second general anaesthetic within half an hour was a very irresponsible procedure, but so was having a bomb falling nearly into your surgery!

During the bombing of London I set off to my London job, more with hope than expectation. It wasn't what you did in those days that mattered, but the fact that you had gone through the motions of trying. "We will not give in" was the catch phrase of the moment. I used to leave home about 7.30 a.m. and, depending upon which roads were usable, reached the Underground Station at Wimbledon South and parked the car. Since the trams and the buses were more or less useless, everyone who could get there used the Tube, though to get on it was a fight to save your backside from "Mind the doors!" It was another squeeze-me-tight affair, but getting off meant you started edging towards the door three stations prior to your destination. You had to get right to the doors so that when they opened you could take the mass on the platform by surprise, so to speak, and before they surged into the train they let you pass through them and out of the station.

The best way to illustrate the mass of humans on the Tubes was to imagine half a dozen sardines trying to get into a full tin, and half a dozen trying to get out. On this particular morning it was The Oval where I had to get off. I did so and went up the escalators to the main entrance, only to find all exit doors shut with railway officials at each door, and never mind what you said, or who you were, you had to stay inside, as there was a raid on and it was chaos outside. "This is your "safest place, mate, so think how lucky you are," was the only consolation offered.

After about an hour of this waiting, I became friendly with another chap who had urgent business to see to, and being shut up like this, bombs or no bombs, was just not good enough. We got together and agreed on a plan to get out. We picked on two shifty-looking chaps and put our plan to them. They would create a disturbance at one door with the attendant, with the intention of making the other railway official move over to help his colleague with the fracas. My friend and I would then nip out of the unguarded door. We dropped these two blokes half a crown and they did their stuff with alacrity.

The plan worked fine and we were outside! - where indeed, there was chaos, with guns blasting off and bombs coming down. We pursued our way, dodging about from cover to cover, but things got so hot at one point that we just dived down some basement steps of a four-storey house in a terrace to take cover. We opened the door and at once found ourselves in the midst of a party of women, sitting round a table drinking tea. They instantly made us welcome with tea and biscuits, and we listened to all their bomb stories until the din ouside abated, and then set off again, half running and half jogging along.

However, within fifteen minutes or so, over came another wave of bombers and down came the bombs again. This time we dived into a Woolworths emporium, straight between two counters, only to find ourselves in the midst of about ten females, all under the counter. We had a hilarious session with this lot and heard all their experiences of war at first hand. Very soon after this second bolt for cover, my friend left me to see if his own Corn Chandlers business was still intact. It struck me as ludicrous in the middle of this upheaval, bombs and fire, to be concerned as to whether your hay loft had gone up in smoke! But perhaps his family were there.

However, on reaching my clinic around 12.45 I was informed by the nurse at the top of the stairs that the back part of the premises had been hit last night and that no one had come for treatment, since the Air Raid Wardens considered the rest of the building unsafe - "But I can make you a cup of tea, Sir. Then you'd better get back home!"

This I did, after a sit down and a bite to eat, fortunately returning home in one and a half hours, whereas my journey in had taken me six and a half hours. I had made the effort and taken the risk, all for nothing.

The bombing continued, and within another month my other two clinics were no more. My services were now transferred to L.C.C. General Hospitals, and here I really was working, since one usually found between thirty and fifty people waiting for treatment in these dental out-patient departments, many of the civilian practices having been demolished by the German bombs raining down on London.

For me, all this was first-class experience in one form or another. In fact, I was faced with a different aspect of dentistry nearly every time I went. My biggest shock was, I think, at St. John's Hospital, Balham, on my second visit. I was met on arrival by the matron and a sister.

"Excuse me, are you the dentist?"

"Yes."

"Please follow me."

She set off at such a cracking pace I had to go up the stairs two-at-a-time. The end of this marathon, down and around the never-ending corridors, finished in a massive ward with about twenty beds on each side, where two white-coated figures waited at the end of a screened-off bed. They were introduced as the surgeons in charge. One, pointing at the screens, said, "Tried to commit suicide by jumping from a block of flats on to a concrete yard. She's still unconscious, most of her bones broken, including her jaw, teeth all over the place. Will you be able to do anything?"

We then went inside the screens and examined by hand the patient's mouth as she lay in a coma. I really did not then know what I was going to do, except to secure her tongue before she swallowed it and choked. I stated this to the assembled party, adding that I must go down to the surgery to get my instruments and would try to remove broken teeth and take impressions for a jaw splint. This prognosis was all very well, but that night I pored over my books as to how I was in fact going to tackle my first broken jaw case.

At these hospital sessions, one found on examination, several patients who needed massive extractions of unsaveable teeth and a general anaesthetic for that operation. The nurse then phoned to the theatre nurse and in due course, the anaesthetist on duty found a place for that dental case or cases. Therefore, no time must be lost in my getting up to the theatre and going into action. The numbers needing help seemed endless, and one was expected to deal with all who came. The pay was the same for five patients or fity-five, and the procedure was understood to be one's 'responsibility'.

The anaesthetic procedure was intravenous (injection direct into the vein). This method I had only witnessed once in my hospital training, and that was by an eminent dental surgeon called Eckner, at a 'Clinical' held in the hospital, and during which, as a senior student, I acted as one of his assistants. It was therefore another new practical experience, and you cannot hope to learn the heart condition of your patient unless you learn to identify the sound the heart and its valves make, either on the arterial or venous side of this amazing human organ, which no man-made engine has yet emulated.

An incident occurred in one anaesthetic case which I have never forgotten. I was just about to start taking out the necessary teeth when the anaesthetist shouted "Wait!" He then put his ear to the patient's heart and asked me to feel his pulse. The patient had in fact given up breathing, and you don't operate in such circumstances. We lifted the unconscious patient off the table on to the theatre floor, and on our hands and knees, turn and turn about, gave our all in artificial repsiration. After nearly twenty minutes there was still no sign of breathing. I then suggested we placed a pillow under his face and chest and worked from the back of his chest, and the miracle happened almost at the anaesthetist's first press down. The engine clicked into motion, and within a few minutes he had risen from the dead.

To say that I was calm and collected would be the understatment of my life. I was dripping wet with perspiration, and soon found myself all of a dither. To crown my immature professional state, I had to rush to the scrubbing-up room and vomit as the full nervous reaction set in. The anaesthetist was more calm and collected, but nevertheless profuse in his thanks to me.

At my next session,when I met him again over a case, he said, "I believe you saved that patient's life last week by your suggestion. If I can show you anything about this intravenous technique, I'll be only too pleased to do so."

I learned more in ten minutes from him than from any text book. Practical example, with the why and the wherefore, is always the most explicit, but it's false confidence. If just watching a dentist extract twenty teeth makes the practice of it as easy as it appears, why do so many dentists send so many cases to surgeon consultants in the hospitals?

The real art of extracting teeth is to learn your own strength in relation to the degree of resistance of the tooth; to recognise this resistance and to take cognisance of it by adopting the appropriate method of leverage. In other words, difficulties are overcome by digital sensitivity to controlled force.

My other early experience of war was at a hospital in Kent, full of the Dunkirk wounded. Many needed dental treatment but were quite unable to come to the surgery, and so I went to treat them in their beds. The best way to do this is quite often to operate from a kneeling position at the side of the bed, using a head lamp on your own head, not a flashlight held in the nurse's hand. My experience with my civilian dentist before I went to hospital helped me here, as he often took me with him when he visited patients in their homes, and I saw how he went about this work. I certainly had no such experience at Dental School, but when I was in the R.A.F. and later in my own practice, I often undertook home treatment.

It was necessary to undergo a medical examination before one's application to join the R.A.F.V.R. was accepted. Mine was due to commence at 10.15 a.m. within the portals of Adastral house, Haymarket, and full of confidence, I joined ten others on that fateful day. About half-way through I was told by the ophthalmic surgeon, on returning to his desk to write his report, "From my examination it appears to me that your left eye is suspect. I regret, therefore that I have to fail you."

"What," I demanded, "is the matter?"

"It is suspect of an early cataract."

With that I rose from the examination chair and went to his desk, and with my fist in his face, said "I suggest you re-examine my eyes, otherwise you could find yourself in trouble!"

After what seemed an age, he got up and came over to give me another testing examination. Then, without going to his desk, I was told that the prognosis was not so definite as he first thought, and that therefore he would not fail me.

I am now seventy-eight and as yet have no cataract in either eye. However, the most amazing thing to me about this medical examination was that, out of the eleven who presented themselves as volunteers, only five were accepted. Within three years, with conscription in full swing, any dentist who could walk was accepted without a quibble. Yet you had to be first class to gain the Volunteer Reserve!

By the irony of fate, or call it what you will, it transpired some three years later, when I was a Senior R.A.F. Dental Surgeon, that a formal request was received via my H.Q. at Hounslow to investigate a report on three local civilian Dental Practitioners in Dumfriesshire who had tried to avoid conscription on the grounds of some medical incapacity for their calling. As a result of my confidential reports, all three had to enlist.

I believe the request for my investigation had come from either the British Dental Association or the Dental Council via my Command R.A.F. Dental H.Q., so one man's meat is in fact another man's poison. Or put another way, Civilian Practice was more appealing than the thought of 18/-d a day.

Late! By carrier pigeon from Christchurch, a reference:

My ex-New Zealand dental nurse, Amanda Dale (née Finny), who came over for the coronation of our Queen, then stayed to work her passage in my Surgery for some seven years. A first-class chairside right hand, since it was there before I opened my mouth, her anticipation learnt the hard way by having done it herself. Amanda left me to get married in the Island of the Long White Cloud.

"It was a happy time whilst in England, to help George Witherwick in his surgery at Chessington, Surbiton, Surrey. George had a sense of humour that always turned potential disasters into something more normal. Furthermore he was quite philosophical about any mistakes I made, giving me confidence. One occasion I remember was when George had to use some pliers to extract the socket of a light bulb, without the current being turned off, causing the pliers in his hand to be flung across the surgery, yet George seemed immune to any harm or ill effect, but seemed rather surprised.

"A feature of this Practice was the fortnightly General Anaesthetic Sessions, with the Anaesthetist Dr John Gordon, when up to six cases were dealt with. When George set to work I had my work cut out counting the teeth which flew at a terrific speed from his nimble forceps. Another feature I remember was his skill in constructing dentures: they never looked false and always stayed where they fitted. George Witherwick's skill in removing impacted wisdom teeth was as remarkable as his chairside manner, often filling the surgery with laughter."

Chapter 6

EARLY R.A.F. AFFAIRS

My Practice was not far away from Epsom, and at Derby time the gipsies were camping wherever they could. However, my first experience of them as patients was during the 'phoney war' in 1940. It would be around 9.15 p.m. when the surgery bell rang, much to my surprise. When I opened the door five gipsies, all women, dressed in black, three of them with heavy black, tasselled shawls, trooped into the waiting room and sat down.

"Are you the surgeon dentist?" the spokeswoman asked.

"Yes," I replied. "Can I help you?"

At this, another stood up and advanced towards me, opened her mouth wide and put her finger on an upper molar tooth. I indicated the surgery and she stepped inside, closely followed by the spokeswoman.

After my examination I explained that an injection was to be given, but at once the spokeswoman demurred.

"She must have no sedation."

"It will be very painful to extract this tooth without an injection," I pointed out.

"It is as nothing to the days and nights of pain she has borne already."

I remonstrated that to remove the tooth without giving an injection would hurt me too, whereupon the elderly spokeswoman came closer and put her hand on my arm.

"We understand, sir, but as we do not believe in sedatives, we must bear our sins as best we can."

She then turned from me and let herself out of the surgery to go into the waiting room, leaving the door open. Soon there came from the room a low incantation or murmuring, which I can only describe as a sort of chant. I was now alone with my dilemma, made worse by observing this poor patient sitting in my dental chair, hands clasped on her lap, with tears falling down her cheeks. I went to my cabinet for the upper tooth forceps, took hold of the patient's clasped hands and clasped them in mine briefly, then placed her head upon the head rest and bade her open her mouth. I applied pressure with the forceps, and luckily the tooth came out without too much difficulty, quickly and in one piece, with not a squeak from the patient.

On taking her back to the waiting room, all four waiting stood up as one. "Thank you sir," said their leader. "What do we owe you?"

"Nothing," I told her. "I'm only sorry I had to hurt her."

As they left the surgery the elderly one turned and said "You will do well here."

I'd never met a true Romany before, nor have I come across any since. But this incident impressed me with their beliefs and steadfast courage to suffer physical pain.

Busy as my practice was, I could never escape the feeling of impermanence, brought about by the constant threat of bombing and my desire to serve in the R.A.F. When the call came, it was with mixed feeling that I closed down the surgery.

My first posting was to Halton, having received an instant commission as Flying Officer from King George VI. I duly reported for duty, arrayed in my uniform, impeccably tailored by Gieves at no small cost to myself.

Our short visit to Halton was solely for the purpose of instruction into the necessary procedures of R.A.F. Dental Branch forms and duties, etc., together with an early morning squad drill; chicken-feed to me as I'd learnt my right from my left when in the Edinburgh University O.T.C. under the auspices of that great Scottish Regiment the Black Watch, and latterly the L.D.V. I was a good shot (Captain of Shooting by Rifle at College and winner of several medals). If I could not extract the tooth from any German prisoner, I could at least shoot him stone dead!

At Halton we Dental Officers were joined by the Volunteer Medical Officers and billeted in a Rothschild mansion, generously put at the disposal of the R.A.F. for the duration and fully staffed by Rothschild retainers. We lived for a short while like Lords and wished we had volunteered before!

After dinner one evening, four of us set off for Aylesbury, and

73

parked the car in what must be one of the largest market squares in the country! We all tripped into The White Horse and did not leave until Time was declared, only to find to our amazement that a real pea-souper had descended. So bad was it that it took at least fifteen minutes to find our car in the square, and another fifteen minutes trying to get the key in the lock. We all tried and failed! The owner of the car, a Dental Surgeon called Gill, in practice at Winchester, called a halt to our endeavours by blandly stating that this was not his car at all!

After a further hiatus we found the right one and all piled in. We set off in the very thick fog, singing at the top of our voices. As it was quite impossible to read any of the signposts, we just left it to the driver and owner of the car to get on with it, until all at once the vehicle came to a grating stop and leant over sideways at an acute angle.

The singing ceased abruptly as we peered out at the mist swirling around us, unable to see a hand before our faces. After a long silence the driver said to the bloke next to him, "You get out and see what's happened."

This chap opened the door, stepped out of the car, and just literally disappeared. There was no sound, no trace - nothing!

The silence within the car became intense. I then said to the man next to me, who was seated behind the one who had disappeared, "Why don't you get out and see what's happened?"

He did so, and he too simply vanished into nowhere. Not a cry nor any sound could we hear in the mist enveloping the marooned car. Whatever the state of intoxication of the driver and myself we were now fully in charge of our faculties!

"What the Hell's going on?" demanded Gill. "You'd better get out on your side and find out."

I borrowed his box of matches and descended carefully, to find I was at least standing on the road. By means of the matches I found my way round the car and along its bonnet to the left front wheel which was hanging over a dark void. I reported back to the driver who then joined me on the edge, from which we both shouted, "Where are you?"

Faintly from the depths a muffled voice came up. "At the bottom of a bloody deep pit, and it's full of water and mud."

To cut a long story short, we eventually got these two out of the pit, and the car being immobilised, we set off on foot to find our way back to Halton in the fog, striking matches at every rustic signpost and eventually reaching Rothschild's home at 6.45 a.m. - plastered up to the eyes in thick mud in our best No. 1 uniforms.

When we returned to change for dinner that evening, these same uniforms were laid out on our beds, all spick and span, as good as new. No paid cleaners could have done it better or quicker.

But where had we been? That was the mystery. After discreet enquiries, all very hush-hush, we learned that we had inadvertently got on to a 'No Entrance' road, which ran alongside a secret tank trap - ordered to be dug around most of London in case the Germans did invade. The two who fell in were lucky to have survived a sheer drop of about eighteen feet without a broken bone between them.

Not long after this, during 1941, I found myself posted to the R.A.F. Recruit Centre for the Women's Auxiliary Air Force, based at Bridgnorth, Shropshire. It was one of the largest dental centres then in the R.A.F., having no less than five surgeries. Dental officers worked morning and afternoon shifts, I mostly with a chap called Hogg, a colleague from my Edinburgh days, and another called Ireland, with somebody else whose name escapes me. We made a fine team.

In overall command as Senior Dental Officer was a Squadron Leader on the regular list, an officious stickler for discipline who made no secret of his disdain for the newly enrolled "civvies" such as myself. Perhaps because I proudly displayed in my lapel the Voluntary Reserve insignia and took no pains to hide my dislike of him, there was no love lost between us.

One morning around 10.30, the Duty Sergeant entered my surgery to announce that Her Royal Highness the Princess Royal, Commandant-in-Chief of the W.A.A.F.s, would be carrying out a formal inspection of the unit at precisely 11.00 a.m. The Squadron Leader wished all officers to stand by their chairs, with no patients in the room.

At 10.45 my next W.A.A.F. came in for treatment, requiring extraction of an upper left second pre-molar. I knew from experience that this tooth often had thin roots, with the apical third bent, making it all too easy to leave a piece of root, difficult to remove so high up in the jawbone. Great care would be needed soon.

A local anaesthetic was injected and the patient sent to a large waiting-room. Meantime I chatted with the nurse about the Squadron Leader, who I said was only half the dentist we graduates from Edinburgh were, and deserved a kick up the backside for his bumptiousness. From what she told me, I gathered she and her colleagues had come to the same conclusion.

The minutes ticked by, and at 11.12 there was still no sign of our Royal Visitor when I popped my head round the door.

"Quick!" I told my nurse. "Fetch that poor girl in. I'll whip her tooth out before the anaesthetic wears off."

The W.A.A.F. came in at the double. We shoved her into the chair, I pushed the probe into her jawbone to ascertain she could feel nothing, and prepared to extract the tooth with the utmost caution, well knowing the chances of breakage. I was actually withdrawing the tooth between the blades of my forceps when the door behind the dental chair opened and my eyes met those of the Princess Royal.

Some impishness made me hold the bloody tooth above the patient's head, the better for the Princess Royal to see. She did not blench but smiled at me and remarked "I've always wanted to see how it's done, and now I know."

Not so impressed was our Squadron Leader standing to the left of her. His face was crimson and he seemed to have difficulty in mouthing my name for a formal introduction. The Princess now spoke to the patient, whose head was in the spittoon, enquiring whether she was all right and did it hurt, to which the girl responded by turning her head to shake it and smile. Reassured, the Princess smiled at us again, waved, and left the surgery.

While I was wondering what the outcome of this unrehearsed scene might be, the heavy footsteps of the sergeant sounded ominously along the corridor and stopped outside the surgery door. "The Squadron Leader wishes to see you in his office, sir, at once," he announced in a voice that could have carried clear across the camp.

I had to keep a tight rein on my temper during the long dressing-down, during which the Senior Dental Officer informed me that he would consult King's Regulations as to my insubordination and disobeying an explicit order. I feared the worst, and at lunchtime at the bar of the mess, the general consensus seemed to be that a Court Martial was awaiting me.

A few week after this, during which time an icy calm characterised the relationship with my superior, I had occasion to spend a long weekend in London. On my return to Wolverhampton, I was devastated to find that another officer had borrowed my car. The car was a 1928 open Austin Seven, known as Waltzing Matilda for its habit of wandering all over the road at any speed beyond 40 m.p.h., due to badly worn front king-pins. Nonetheless I was familiar with its funny little ways, and the twelve pounds I had paid the anaesthetist for it seemed good value.

Failing to find any trace of the car, I telephoned the Squadron Leader at Bridgnorth to tell him I would be reporting late for duty. The reply was distinctly frosty. Unless I was back in the Dental Centre by 2 p.m. sharp, he would consider it a dereliction of duty calling for serious action against me. It was obvious that the little matter of the Princess Royal's visit still rankled with him, and when he abruptly put down the receiver I knew he was gunning for me.

I had intended to take the bus from Wolverhampton to Bridgnorth, but there was no time now. I dashed off to the nearest taxi rank and shouted "Can anyone get me to Bridgnorth by 2 o'clock?"

Somebody called out that he would try. I jumped into the taxi and explained my plight, at which the man grinned sympathetically. "It normally takes forty minutes," he said. "Today it's going to be thirty. Hold-on!"

I did so, and we began our sixty-miles-an-hour dash to beat the deadline. I then realised I was short of money and shouted to him that I might have to pay him later.

"Have you got a couple of quid?" he yelled back.

"Yes."

"That'll do. You can buy me a drink one day."

We arrived before 2 p.m., and I bounced into the S.D.O.'s office with a minute or two to spare. "Reporting for duty, sir," I shouted triumphantly, giving the regulation salute.

He scowled and said nothing, but a week or two later he had his revenge. Instead of my requested posting to Cornwall, he sent me to Stranraer, which was about as far from Cornwall as anybody could devise. But before leaving Bridgnorth, I must mention an amusing incident concerning this car.

When I sold 'Waltzing Matilda' for £14 to Charlie Hogg, giving me £2 clear porfit, everyone knew about it. The day following the sale, Charlie took the wheel of his first car, with myself and two colleagues, all in No. 1 uniform. With the Guard turned out at the entrance, we swept out like royalty, watched by crowds of service personnel. We had barely gone fifty yards down the road towards Bridgnorth, when the car gave a sudden lurch to its near side and slid over, throwing its passengers out on to the road, and finishing up 'arse over tip' with its engine still running. We picked ourselves up, luckily unharmed, and rushed to the car, lifted it bodily back on to its wheels, and stopped the engine. The left front wheel had dropped off!

Walking back along the road, amidst shouts of derision and cat calls, we found the wheel and also the king pin, which had fallen out of the hub. This was soon re-fixed. The windscreen was forced back into its original position, the engine re-started, and off we went again, only to find that Charlie, now in a raging temper with me, could not get the steering to turn left. It would only move the wheels to the right. We then had no choice but to follow right hand turns all the way round to get to a garage in Bridgnorth.

I regret to say that it was some considerable time before Charlie reconciled himself to the fact that I had not sold him the car knowing the wheel was going to fall off. As I repeatedly pointed out, if I had known this was going to happen, what was I doing risking my life sitting in the back of it? After this episode, the car became even more famous.

I had sold the car because a friend of mine in Wolverhampton, who ran an engineering factory, had kindly offered me a vintage Wolseley Hornet, which was lying about in one of his factory sheds. At £5 it was too good to miss.

This was the car that my wife came to know so well. She had joined me at Bridgnorth, to live out at Tedstill Farm, having let our house unfurnished and stored all our furniture in the surgery waiting room. As it turned out, the small income from this source was most welcome. My pay as a Flying Officer in no way compared with my earnings in dentistry, and as I was under 30, I did not qualify for married allowances, so that Audrey and I had to live off-camp in what was politely called 'reduced circumstances'. Indeed, during the first year or so, and before I was promoted, we had several times to ask a friend to go into the surgery, find something saleable stored among our belongings, and take it on the bus to Surbiton, sending the proceeds to us in Scotland. So much for volunteering!

The folk at this farm were very nice people, and we soon made friends. We arrived with our Sealyham dog, Tuppence, which had previously belonged to Anna Neagle as a puppy, together with a lovely ginger cat. This latter animal was so happy on the farm that when we left for the posting to Stranraer, he conveniently lost himself with no intention of leaving the place.

Our kind friends at Tedstill insisted, just prior to my departure for Scotland, that we must have a Sunday day out as a farewell gesture, and visit his brother's farm. We arrived mid-afternoon, and leaving the ladies to their own devices, our host took us down into the cellar below the farmhouse to sample his home made cider. We went from barrel to barrel as we sampled glass after glass, which to me seemed a pretty innocuous sort of drink.

After tea, our host suggested a trip to the local for a 'quickie' before I drove my party back to Tedstill. Well, we had several 'quickies' in this pub, but when I emerged I suddenly found myself more drunk than sober. The whisky and beer, together with the strong home-brewed cider, just about pole-axed me.

That drive back home some twenty five miles, was the most hazardous I've ever undertaken. I was not concerned with the traffic - there was none - but mainly to keep the vehicle on the road and out of the ditch. Added to which, I received no help from my farmer friend who kept urging me to to greater speed, implying that I could not drive very well at all, to the great consternation of our respective wives in the back, who were sober but scared stiff. At one stage, my wife even declared that she was going to report me to the C.O. for being drunk whilst driving. Happily we all arrived safely with my reputation intact.

Our journey in the Hornet from Bridgnorth to Stranraer was quite an epic that occupied all day and night and most of the next day. I had acquired a builder's second-hand trailer to fix behind the car to carry our main bits and pieces. The two were hitched up together with a six inch nail as a bolt. We made pretty good progress until we hit Wigan, where the roads had just been freshly tarred but due to the very hot weather, this sparsely-covered tar was molten, and the trailer was consequently swinging about left to right all over the road. We got out of the town as quickly as possible! It was probably this excessive swinging about that led to the calamity while going over Shap into Scotland.

We had stopped for a square meal before ascending the very steep, long hill and then, feeling more asleep than awake, dozed for a few hours. The climb over Shap started about 4.00 a.m. with the dawn just breaking and the mist still quite dense. There was of course nothing else on the road, with petrol strictly rationed.

The steep incline, together with the weight of the trailer, caused the car to make heavy weather, but half way up, the car suddenly seemed to gather strength, as if it was now working on all cylinders, and reached the top in fine fettle. When I stopped to relieve myself, I was horrified to discover that we had no trailer! Oh yes, I found it! Half-way into a field, having swung off the road and run back into a four foot stone wall! When I came upon it through the mist, several sheep were also investigating its presence. It was no easy job to back down Shap and link up again with my trailer - especially as the linking-pin was nowhere to be seen. I happened to have a pretty stout screw-driver and that became the new pin - would it hold? It did, and on into Scotland we went, ultimately arriving at Glenluce, at the head of Luce Bay, about 6.00 p.m.

George aged three with stick.

George aged seven on the running board of the Moon Car in the drive of his father's house at Overstrand, Newland Park, Hull; used in the trip to London to see the Wembley Exhibition in 1926.

(R to L) George, his father and John Leech at Scarborough, about 1922.

Christmas display at George's father's fish, game and poultry shop in Hull (mid 1930s).

John o' Groats Jetty, 1938: Fishermen busy transferring lobsters just landed in boat to boxes, which are left in the sea to keep fish fresh till they are ready for transport to London. Audrey a spectator on left, Stroma behind.

Typical R.A.F. dental surgery, World War II.

George assisting the Queen Mother at the tree planting ceremony on the occasion of her Majesty's opening the Duchy Hospital, Truro (1983).

Viscountess Falmouth planting a tree to mark the opening of
Trelean Valley Garden (1983).

George and Audrey's Golden Wedding celebrations at Nansloe Manor in 1988.

A recent photograph of George at Trelean.

Chapter 7

FANGS

The posting was actually at West Freugh, a lovely unit well hidden on a moor, and with a delighful First World War mess. Our first lodgings were nearby at Carescrew, a 3,000 acre sheep farm run by John Murray. It used to take him all day to patrol the hills to tend his flock. These West Highland sheep had long curling horns and the tups had them twice as big. At dipping-time it took three men to deal with each. One sat behind its head, one faced the other way sitting on its hind quarters, whilst the third, armed with hand clippers and a sharp knife, clipped the hair from under the vicious horns to expose the skin and a seething mass of maggots, a revolting sight. The whole lot was cut out until healthy tissue was exposed and this doused with Stockholm tar. The animal was then shoved into the dip.

The 'Gathering' went on for the best part of the week, farmers coming from all around to lend a hand. Murray ran the farm and, with the hired help, managed the milking herd of Ayrshire cows. But far away, hidden by hills and completely wild, was a herd of black Galloways. If you went anywhere near them, they all advanced towards you, snorting with tails up - you had to be a man-and-a-half to deal with this herd.

We subsequently managed to get cheaper lodging at a delightful cottage at the head of Luce Bay, Glenluce, Wigtownshire. The Bents cottage had no water, no electricity, rats in the thatch and a bucket privy. It was a mile-and-a-half from the village, with the beach at the front and only door.

One morning on my five-mile run to the camp in my old £5 car, scuttling along the narrow high-hedged road, my attention was drawn to a Tiger Moth aeroplane flying with me along the top of the hedge, with the C.O. leaning out pointing to his wrist watch and shouting, "See me in the mess at lunch, Fangs. What's your tipple? You'd better get a faster car."

Group Capain Openshaw was stout, jolly, rosy-cheeked, well liked by everyone, and with his ginger hair universally known as 'Ginger' Openshaw.

While I was stationed here I was given two satellite units to look after. One, at Castle Kennedy, was just being created within the ample acres of the Earl of Stair's place. Except for the wooden building at the entrance which did duty as the Guard Room, C.O.'s office and W.O.I.'s stamping ground, everything else was tented. After some difficulty I found my Dental Unit, set within pine treets, a neat, small bell tent, complete with camp stool, bucket, jug and water, and first aid, pattern-type forceps, with all accountrements necessary.

One really learnt the art of dentistry using foot drills, and what resembled army-type forceps. Bowls and jugs of water and buckets were there to spit into after you had dealt with the offending tooth, and then told the long-suffering A.C.II to close the flap as he went out. I have always considered I qualified for overseas pay on this satellite unit, but I never got it!

The best part of the assignment was to be able to wander amongst the lovely gardens of this beautiful estate, especially the rhododendrons, luxuriating in the mild, humid atmosphere that is a feature of Wigtownshire with its other lovely gardens at Logan.

My next move was to an Advanced Flying Unit at Torthorwald near Lochmaben which, in order to continue its flying training, mainly night flying for bomber crews, had moved up quickly from Essex, where its activities had been curtailed by the German day bombing raids. In Dumfriesshire it was difficult to realise that there was a war in progress. The main problem when I arrived was the fact that the staff pilots seemed to be unable to keep the twin-engined training aeroplanes airborne when one engine cut out. It was becoming a major problem of national importance. If you can't get your bomber trainees airborne, they won't learn the job anywhere else.

It was soon after my arrival as Dental Officer in charge, that the Senior Medical Officer suggested we visit the Unit Mortuary. I cannot describe what I saw, nor the stench, but it was all part of the price being paid in human lives to keep these aircraft flying when one engine failed. The bits and pieces of human endeavour were all in here, being sorted out to fit into coffins, carrying the name tag and citation 'Died on Active Service'.

Somebody in the Air Council had a shaft of inspiration in the person of Joe King. He arrived to take charge of the unit in a most surreptitious manner. No one seemed to know where the C.O. had gone or who the new one was. I remember phoning to speak to the adjutant, only to be told by somebody that there was no adjutant. "What do you mean?" I said.

"He's been sacked, posted and gone, and so there ain't one. Who's that speaking?"

It seemed diplomatic not to pursue the enquiry.

Joe King, it subsequently came down to us, had more or less taken charge of flying control. He wasted no time in taking up each individual staff pilot in their dicey machines to show them what flying was really about. Cutting out one engine, he proceeded to demonstrate how to keep the craft flying on the remaining one and land it safely.

Within three weeks the atmosphere in that flying unit was transformed by the presence of this one man, Group Captain (later Air Commodore) Joe King, ex-Canadian Air Force retired, A.F.C., D.F.C and Bar. I, a mere dental officer, saluted and deeply respected him.

However, I discovered that this remarkable man had a further skill to admire. He was nudging sixty, had come out of retirement from the backwoods of Canada, and lived out on a farm, four or five fields away from where Audrey and I had rented a cottage with a nine-acre smallholding, Parkfoot Lochmaben. I ran this in my spare time for the next three and a half years with some 150 chickens, a pig, two dozen ducks, a goat, turkeys, three cats and two Sealyham dogs, Tuppence and Jenny. I also had a tennis-court-size vegetable garden from which I supplied the messing officer with whatever I could grow.

One day, when I was on a week's leave, in walked Joe King, now in battle dress, "Oh, sorry to interfere with your leave," he apologised. "I wondered if you and your wife would care to come over to May Erskine's place, about 11.30 this morning, as I'm bringing down three trees." My interest in trees was well-known.

The three wych-elms were growing out of a hedge between fields, and were each well over a hundred feet in height with trunks five feet across. There was a party of three or four other people there when we arrived and Group Captain King addressed us. Pointing to three stakes set in the ground, he said, "These trees are almost ready to fell. I hope to drop them as near to the stakes as possible."

He did just that, two slap on the stake and the third two feet away, and all he used on those massive boles was his axe; no saw and no wedges. Apparently on leaving the Canadian Air Force he had bought an area of high timber, built a shack, and during the spring and summer spent most of his time felling the timber. It is an activity rarely seen in this country, and I was fascinated to see it done by an expert. The modern chain-saw demands no such skill.

One day Joe King appeared in my Dental Centre just on lunch-time, coming through the waiting room into the surgery. With his hand on the front door knob he addressed me thus: "This linoleum requires renewal. Go to the stores and get new stuff laid down this afternoon. I'll call in at 4.30 to see if it's all in place."

With that he left. The job took all the afternoon and the assistance of medical orderlies, my nurses and the storemen, whom I ordered to stay and help after they had delivered the linoleum on the handcart. Joe King did not in fact appear at 4.30. He knew that the new linoleum would be in place.

Shortly after that I went to S.H.Q. to see him. When the adjutant announced my presence, Joe King shouted through, "Show Fangs in."

"Come and sit here," he greeted me as I entered. "I'm dealing with the defaulters."

When the next one came in, escorted by the Station Warrant Officer, the Commanding Officer listened to the charge and then turned to me. "Well, Fangs, what do you reckon we should do with him?"

I stood up and went towards the defaulter. "I'm the Dental Officer. Open you mouth."

I quickly spotted some trouble with his teeth and returned to my seat by the C.O.

"Well, Sir," I said, "I would suggest this man report dentally sick tomorrow morning for treatment."

"Well done, Fangs," replied the C.O. "That's the ticket. You give him Hell! Next defaulter!"

When the defaulters had been dealt with, the adjutant came in with the mail that he considered his superior should deal with. One letter was from an irate lady in Dumfries, complaining of our night flying, night after night, interfering with her sleep. "Now Fangs," said the C.O. "What's your answer to that?"

"Well Sir," I said, after some thought, "You could point out to this lady that whilst we regret keeping her awake, it is only by training our own Scottish airmen in the area of night flying that we can hope to keep the German people of Berlin awake all and every night."

"Excellent, Fangs," he congratulated me. "Adjutant, get that lot typed for me to sign."

Another incident that I recollect vividly was far from amusing. I was in my surgery when, just before lunch,the Senior Medical Officer came running in. "Sorry to disturb you, Fangs, I've just come from Dumfries Infirmary. Wing Commander Burt has been taken there in a bad way. I think there's something wrong with his jaw that you should look at."

We set off at once. The Wing Commander was certainly in trouble. His jaw was smashed, but worse still he was flat on his back, coughing and almost choking, with his tongue curling back and threatening to block his throat. I made sure somebody stayed with him before going in search of the Sister. She was at lunch, so I rummaged through her table drawer until I found a needle and thread. Armed with this I returned to the patient, now semi-conscious. Holding his slippery tongue between my fingers and a clean handkerchief, I managed to force the darning needle through the tongue. I then tied a surgeon's knot in the thread and fixed the other end to the bed-sheet, which was tucked under the mattress at such a distance that his tongue could not fall back down his throat and choke him. The jaw having been fractured in two places across the mid-line and about the first molar meant that the piece of tissue under the tongue and fixed to the inside of the lower jaw was no longer stable. Lying on his back, the tongue could very easily curl back and choke him.

As everybody seemed to be at lunch and there was no sign of any surgeon, I went straight back to my R.A.F. Unit and into the mess to find the S.M.O. to join him for lunch, relating what had happened to the Wing Commander. "I've secured his tongue," I said. "But it's no good having him flat on his back in that place. He's got to be removed and taken as soon as possible to the maxilla facial unit outside Edinburgh. It's bloody urgent. I can't sort his jaw out. I'm not trained for that. But it's up to me to get him as quickly as possible to where it can be properly seen to."

"Right, Fangs," was the reply. "You can have the ambulance. We'll both go, after lunch, to get the C.O.'s permission to drive him straight to this special jaw unit at Edinburgh."

"I'll go with him in the ambulance and make sure he's sitting up all the way," I promised.

Joe King listened to me and, with the S.M.O. giving moral support, said in his Canadian drawl, "We must look after the Wing Commander. He's worth half the unit. But what the hell are you going by road for? Fetch him out of the Infirmary, fly him to Edinburgh and get transport from there to this special hospital. You go with him, Fangs. He's your responsibility."

What Group Captain Joe King said went, and we duly embarked upon a very hectic and bumpy ride in that plane. I had to spend all the time kneeling on the floor by the patient, trying to keep the support of pillows and empty ammunition boxes so that his back and head were kept upright. This was particularly difficult as the aeroplane was being blown about like a cork over those never-ending Cheviot Hills, all covered in snow, while inside the plane it was icy cold and breezy as the peaks below, and noisy enough to split your eardrums.

We landed at Turnhouse, Edinburgh, the first touchdown throwing me against the side of the aircraft, and Wing Commander Burt flat on his back, luckily with my needle and thread, now fixed to his pyjamas, holding his tongue safe. Outside in the teeth of a blizzard we somehow manoeuvred our patient into the ambulance waiting on the grass runway with me still holding his head up. At least the journey to the hospital unit was more comfortable than that awful flight.

The biggest surprise to me in the whole incident was at about 8.30 p.m., having put our charge into a nice bed with a proper back support, with no fear of tongue swallowing, when in walked John Bond, one of my former House Surgeons at Edinburgh. Needless to say we had much to talk about over our meal, and I very much appreciated the invitation to join him in the theatre to watch him operate upon Wing Commander Burt's double fracture of the mandible that night. John Bond was the surgeon in charge of this specialised unit, the only one then in Scotland and the far North of England, dealing mainly with head and neck injuries, especially those involving the upper and lower jaws. He later became Professor John Bond, and later still Dean of the Dental Faculty, R.C.S. Edinburgh.

The outcome of all this was not only a satisfactory recovery for Wing Commander Burt, who was able to return to full duty within three months to take charge of the flying wing of the Unit. Out of the blue I received an invitation from Command H.Q. to attend a three week course at East Grinstead, Sussex, on maxilla facial operations;

86

all facets of head and neck injuries, restorations of facial contours, skin and bone grafts, under the active control and supervision of that most eminent surgeon Sir John MacKindoe. I was indeed fortunate, as it was the most inspiring and interesting three weeks of dental surgery I ever spent. I shared some delightful lodgings in a private house, the back rooms of which look across country to Ashdown Forest, with a very charming and generous hostess. At night, after dinner, John Phillips from Bristol and my house colleague usually foregathered in a well known public house and chatted with others on the course, mostly Australians and Americans as well as Canadians, and thus learnt a good deal of the kind of dentistry these boys did in their own back yards.

One fact stood out. We British seemed to be jacks of all trades in our profession, whilst all these other dental chaps seemed to specialise in only one department of our science. Furthermore, we who practised all aspects of our trade and did not even consider ourselves specialists were referred to as plain 'Mr.', whereas these specialists, clever no doubt as they were in only one branch or section of dentistry, were collectively referred to as Doctors. There are probably more 'Doctors' in the U.S.A. and other parts of the far flung British Empire that was, than the number of patients they treated! British Dental Surgeons are an anachronism of a bygone era, and those in the R.A.F. stuck with the universal nickname of 'Fangs'; hardly a professional title.

While under Joe King's command at Torthorwald I was fully stretched, responsible for the dental health of some 6,000 service personnel, from the humblest ACII to the 'Scrambled Egg' fraternity at Group Headquarters. My pleas for assistance went unheeded for two years, when another and more corpulent Edinburgh Graduate arrived, by name Roger White. We became quite friendly. At about the same time, I also came to know well a young airman from Kenya, Louis Van 'Aardt. What stamped him as different from the British servicemen was his perpetual sunny smile and a willingness to tackle anything. Whatever the chore, he would find a way to do it effectively and cheerfully. Enthusiasm glowed in his face. he had volunteered, had set his heart on Aircrew service, and qualified as an Air Gunner or 'tail end Charlie'.

Before he went to join his Bomber Squadron he came for a dental examination, at which everything was dealt with except one item. To this I did the Nelson trick of closing one eye. Please do not think I was incompetent. No. I closed my eye to something that might cause intense trouble and pain, but just when, was an unknown factor. I, as most of the dental profession would have done in the circumstances, backed off and hoped that if it did blow up, it would be someone else who had to deal with it! I noticed he had a suspicious unerupted lower third molar, and had all his other teeth present on that side of the mouth. Although I had seen such impacted wisdom teeth removed at hospital by the experts in that field, I had never even been allowed to try. On the two occasions when I had begun, in the General Anaesthetic Room at Edinburgh, I was pulled out almost at once by Johnstone Brown, the Surgeon in Charge, so like everyone else I backed off it. Let sleeping dogs lie!

About this time (1942) the first batch for the Empire Training Scheme was coming in. These, the flower of Canada, Australia, South Africa, New Zealand, Southern Rhodesia, and the rest, were all in their twenties, and volunteers to a man. Four hundred of those fine men were arriving every five weeks for an intensive course, especially night flying, before being posted to their Bomber Squadrons.

What had this to do with me? Quite a lot in fact. An Air Council memorandum came to me, via my H.Q. at Hounslow, to the effect that these Empire Boys were to be made dentally fit as a priority class before proceeding to active stations. I put on another pair of skates and got cracking. It was my job, and that was all there was to it. Fortunately the Empire men were by and large in very good dental health, but every one was carefully examined and treated, except for those with suspect impacted lower wisdoms.

One day I received a letter from Louis Van 'Aardt's wife in Bournemouth. Had I any news of Louis? Nothing had been heard about him since his Lancaster had taken part in the then biggest raid on Berlin some five weeks ago. We could only hope he had survived and was a prisoner. Later came the fateful card from his wife via the Red Cross. He was safe and well, having nearly made it to sanctuary in Spain, but had been forced to give himself up, as he was suffering intense pain from his teeth.

This hit me like a physical blow. I could not sleep for the worry of it all. I knew where the pain had come from. I could see the *very tooth* as I went about my daily work. It was my responsibility and I had funked it. As a result, Louis had been forced to give up his escape effort due to the unbearable pain, and was now locked up for the rest of the war.

In the end I went to see the S.M.O. and told him how I felt and what I intended to do. Squadron Leader R. Witt, M.D., gave me his full support. My intention was simply to operate on all suspected unerupted lower wisdom teeth found when I examined each batch of Empire Aircrew and to begin forthwith. The main problem was in creating time to do it. I therefore asked my only nurse Miss Crone Youghal, as I intended to go back to the surgery, three nights a week for two hours after five-thirty, in other words to work a full day, and on three days do two hours extra after the tea break, when normally I finished and went home. The actual operations on these wisdom teeth would be undertaken between 11.00 and 1.00 p.m. on two days each week.

Due to my lack of experience in the special technique of dealing with impacted teeth, I unfortunately caused a lot of after-pain, so to mitigate this I put such difficult cases into sick quarters for several days. I am afraid my dental efforts for these aircrews made me a detested person. Nobody appreciates being made to have an operation for something that is causing no pain; still worse, having had the operation to suffer a lot of pain and inability to eat anything except with difficulty - and also be taken off training for several days.

Explaining that I was undertaking this operation purely as a preventative of possible pain as a prisoner and being operated upon perhaps by a German dentist was not very sympathetically received. However I drove myself to undertake this radical treatment - convinced by the fate that befell Louis Van 'Aardt that doing what my conscience dictated was simply my duty and responsibility. Furthermore there was no one else better qualified for the work, since I was the Senior Dental Officer and the only one. I was also standing in at the Dumfries Infirmary as Consultant Dental Surgeon to deal with any special case referred by civilian dentists. The more cases I undertook, the better skilled I became and the less after-pain the patients had to suffer, but to begin with it was a clear cut case of "being cruel to be kind".

They never knew about all this back at Hounslow where my chiefs were, and my extra work went on for over a year until my assistant arrived to man another surgery.

Before all this wisdom tooth business arose I was involved with a serious outbreak in the unit of Trench Mouth, or ulcerative stomatitis. This is a painful condition affecting the gums, cheeks and throat, so much so that sufferers cannot swallow food. They run a temperature and generally feel rotten. So bad did this condition become, that in conjunction with the S.M.O. I went to see the C.O. and requested that my remedies of prevention be put into operation, one of which was by placing the town of Dumfries out of bounds to all ranks. The condition is very infectious, and drinking beer or cups of tea, or what have you, can leave the causative bacteria on the drinking utensil if not properly washed up. On the camp I organised large galvanised tubs outside the messes and had R.A.F. Regiment guards posted by the containers so that everyone had to wash their mugs, knives and forks in the chlorinated fluid.

It took five weeks to overcome the outbreak, and in consequence a special seminar of Dental Officers from all over the country was organised and I was called to Hounslow to deliver an address on the steps taken. I also had to write a report on my procedures, and this was circulated throughout the entire Dental Section of the R.A.F.

Audrey and I managed to keep busy in our own lives, and although she longed for her own home, she rarely complained. The social life compensated somewhat for the dull months of service routine away from most of the action. My love of dentistry led me to experiment with the implantation of teeth in 1943, a subject I shall only touch upon at this stage, and which some people in need of specialist dental treatment would shy away from, even today. It all comes down to the fear of being hurt, and I have often found that the biggest and toughest looking individuals can be reduced to abject cowards in the dentist's chair. Fear is no respecter of persons, as the following anecdote will show.

One day during my service career, the Station Padre came to see me. In the chair I examined his teeth and found one that needed filling. I explained that an injection would be advisable, and he agreed. Before I could withdraw my fingers from his mouth, he had clamped his jaws together and his teeth met on one of my fingers. The pain was excruciating. Normally a patient would have realised what he was doing and let go. No so the Padre. His teeth were locked on my finger as though hanging on for dear life. I could stand it no longer.

"Padre," I said in a commanding tone. "I presume you will need your tongue on Sunday for your sermon. I need my finger right now, if you please."

He relaxed his jaws immediately, and when to his evident surprise he saw that his teeth had penetrated to the bone of my finger, his apologies were profuse. He had not been aware of anything untoward, and his jaws had closed on my finger in an unconscious reflex action brought about by sudden terror.

Those of my readers who have visited a dentist may find it difficult to imagine others whose teeth give them no trouble. But this is the case with many primitive peoples and particularly those of the African races. In Great Britain, like other so-called civilised countries, modern foods and eating habits have played havoc with the teeth's natural defences, ensuring a busy time for any qualified dentist. So it was refreshing, in the part of Scotland I was familiar with, to come across a grand old man working his seven-acre smallholding near Lochmaben. We got into conversation, and I was surprised to learn that he was eighty-seven. "What do you do in the R.A.F., young man?" he enquired.

"I'm a Dental Officer."

Thereupon he opened his mouth wide. "Are these all right?" he asked, pointing in.

Amazingly, he appeared to have a full set of teeth. Not only that, there was no sign at all of any decay. "Excellent," I conceded. "Absolutely fine."

"Never once had toothache," he said with deserved satisfaction, "and you're the first dental man I've ever met. Tell me, which part of England are you from?"

"Near London," I replied.

He nodded wisely. "Ah, London. Yes, I've heard tell of the place."

It was said without a trace of hesitation or insincerity. Apparently he had lived his long life in blissful ignorance of the most famous capital city in the world.

While we were tucked away a million miles, it seemed, from the war, the tide had turned in favour of the Allies. The Second Front had established a bridgehead on the Continent, and the Axis powers were being squeezed from East and West in a giant pincer movement that ended in the conflagration of Berlin, the death of Hitler and the collapse of all armed resistance. The struggle for Europe was ended. VE Day, the term coined by the Press, was greeted by jubilation all over the British Isles. To celebrate the news I collected a party, filled my old car to capacity, drove it on to the airfield and went full pelt up and down both runways, then all round the perimeter track, all of us yelling at the top of our voices. It was one of the most memorable and emotional experiences of my life. Within a matter of weeks the entire unit was ordered to move to Oxfordshire, to a unit near Banbury, but the crux of the matter was that the operation had to be carried out within 72 hours. It meant that each officer who was in charge of whatever section within the station had to make his own arrangements and organise everything himself, including transportation.

This was a pretty tall order. I had no transport and the whole of one surgery's equipment to shift with only two assistants, both female nurses. Fortunately one of the girls had a boy friend in M.T. (Motor Transport section), who acquired a lorry and helped me to strip the surgery and load it all. He then drove the vehicle from Dumfries to Banbury, I following in my car with the more fragile equipment and one nurse, a medical orderly, and another mechanic from M.T. I made a detour from the Great North Road to see my father in Hull and my friend John Leech, and then pushed on for Banbury. We unloaded and set everything up, and I was able to phone my C.O. at Hounslow at 5.00 p.m. on the third day that we were fully operational in our new surgery at R.A.F. Chipping Warden, all shipshape and Bristol fashion.

I went back some five weeks later to fetch my wife and shut down my smallholding, the worst part of which was to shoot our three cats. It was the kindest thing to do, and it hurt me more than it did them. I sold my hens and ducks for thirty pounds more than the gratuity I was later generously granted by the Labour Government, which after five and a half years was £147.

Meantime service life continued mush as before, though now we knew that it was only a matter of time before the Japanese were defeated and we could return to civilian life. While at Chipping Warden I met with some interesting situations that called for a certain delicacy of touch. In particular I recall having a visit from the local medical practitioner or GP, who sought my professional help. When we adjourned to the Officers Mess, I established that his problem concerned a young lady living in the depths of the country nearby who was scared stiff of having her teeth seen to, etc.

"But why come to see me?" I asked the doctor. "There are plenty of dentists in Banbury or Leamington."

"Ah! yes," he said, "but the trouble is caused by an unerupted wisdom tooth, and you appear to be something of an expert in this department."

So I went to see the lady in trouble, with the doctor in attendance. Sure enough it was an unerupted lower left wisdom, and what's more, infected. Happily I had advised this very charming young lady through her doctor to hold plenty of very hot water laced with Sanitas or T.C.P. at the back of her mouth at frequent intervals. This I had prophesied would give some relief before morning. It did, and my standing as a dental witch doctor was much enhanced. The doctor wished me to undertake the removal of this tooth within the surgery of the R.A.F., but this I felt she was unable to do as she was in no way connected with the R.A.F. and the whole of station sick quarters would know, and therefore the entire Unit! It would have to be done in her own home.

One evening about 6.00 p.m. we assembled at a rather grand house, she installed in an armchair in the drawing room, with Willie Eardley-Wilmot, the estate agent, alternately holding a flashlight with the doctor, while her husband paced up and down as if she were giving birth to her first-born. Fortune shines on the brave they say and everything went like clockwork, much to my satisfaction. I was playing with fire in undertaking such a major and hazardous operation under the worst of conditions, knowing full well that I was out on a limb if anything serious had gone wrong. When it was all over, great relief and much jollity spread through that drawing room. The whisky flowed, we talked incessantly, and the doctor amazed us by bursting into song in some foreign language. I left bearing a very large bottle of Scotch as a grateful memento of a happy evening.

Two further postings were to round off my service career; to Stormy Down (near Bridgend, South Wales) and Sealand in Cheshire. At the first, the camp seemed overrun by Free French and Polish personnel. On the face of it, it should have been no harder to treat these patients than British ones. But the Poles were a law unto themselves. They would not attend the surgery for inspection and treatment, and always offered the same excuse; a shaking of the head, a blank stare, and gestures to indicate that they didn't understand what was said.

I persevered until I reached an impass. Without their co-operation, I could not do my job. Then I remembered that name of a Polish Officer, English-speaking, whom I had met at Chipping Warden. To my telephone request for guidance he responded positively. He would arrange an appointment with the Polish Personnel Officer at Stormy Down, and explain what was required in a language the men would understand.

Within days he had done just that, and I had no further problem with treating the Poles.

In peacetime, the camaraderie that in war welds together all ranks in a joint effort gives way to other considerations. Individual duties are more sharply defined, as are the gradations of rank. Rank and promotion become the main preoccupation of officers and N.C.O.'s, and the attendant privileges are fiercely defended. Nowhere was this more obvious than at Stormy Down on the occasion of the visit by the R.A.F. Chief Dental Officer. This VIP, and Air Commodore, was in my charge from the moment he arrived.

I made all the necessary arrangements to show him round the extensive Dental Centre, which had no fewer than seventeen personnel in its establishment, including four officers and a Sergeant i/c. The first place I took him to was the C.O.'s office, having previously alerted the Adjutant. To my surprise, the Commanding Officer was not available.

We then toured the Medical Section, from where I telephoned the Adjutants to say that we were on our way to see the C.O., and set off to do so. On arrival, we found once again that he was 'not available'.

I was feeling very frustrated. We had seen the Medical Section and the Dental Centre but still not the man in overall command of the Station. Heaven knows how it looked to the Air Commodore!

We adjourned to the Mess for an early tea and general discussion, after which my VIP was ready to leave. For the third time we danced attendance on the C.O., to be informed once more that he was not available. My visitor departed, I suspect with some interesting views on Station Commanders!

This gratuitous insult had come about simply because the Air Commodore was superior in rank to the Commanding Officer, who therefore declined to meet him as an inferior on his own stamping-ground.

Promotion, at least in the R.A.F., throws up all sorts of anomalies. I remember being made up to Squadron Leader and my pleasure in it, but not for long. Instead of being able to settle down where I was, in my new rank, I was pulled out of the Command and posted to Maintenance Command. Why? Because there was no Squadron Leader establishment in my own Command. Likewise a Flight Sergeant can't hold his rank unless there are a certain number of other ranks under him. The end result of this game of musical chairs is that often the chap who deserves promotion does not get it. The Awards system produces similar injustices. A certain number of minor decorations are agreed by the authorites, to be shared among the various sections of the Service. If you happen to be in the right place at the right time, and your job is one for which an Award may be appropriate, all you have to do is to be there when the gongs are being handed out. The fact that the previous incumbent of that post may have had a blameless career of the highest merit is neither here nor there. So it is with the Civil Service. No matter how much you may deserve recognition, if you're not on the spot to receive it, you don't get your O.B.E. or whatever. Twice in my life I have been told I was in line for some small recognition, and for the reasons above, failed on both occasions to achieve it.

With my next and last posting to Sealand I exchanged one set of problems for another. Here I was responsible for 7,000 people with an establishment of five Dental Officers and staff complement, but found myself with one male orderly and one nurse receptionist. With so many leaving the service on demobilisation, my own release was put back until a replacement could be found. This set me back three months in which time I had pause to reflect that my short stay had presented me with more administrative problems than the whole of my service career until then. Every day brought some minor or petty difference to my door for decision and action. It seemed as though the more people you were responsible for, the greater the number of petty complaints that required your attention and took you away from the dental work you had been trained for. When my replacement finally arrived at 11.00 a.m. during a Sick Parade that normally lasted until lunch-time, I could not wait to go. Flinging off my white coat and donning the uniform jacket, I led the newcomer to the office of the Senior Medical Officer and introduced him, then made my farewells to all concerned, and with my car stuffed full of personal belongings, drove straight to Uxbridge for demobilisation and the comparative luxury of a civilian suit. Within seventy-two hours of arriving at my home in Surrey I had reopened the surgery. It was back to "business as usual."

Chapter 8

CIVVY STREET

Although the civilian life I returned to in 1947 was very different from the one I had left, it was a time to be thankful. Where many families had lost their breadwinner and close relatives on active service or as victims of the bombing, Audrey and I had come through unscathed. The house in Hurst Road, Bexley, where I had lodged before the war while waiting for Audrey to join me in my first practice, had been totally destroyed by a bomb. Oddly, it was the only house in the road to be hit, and it gave me a strange feeling to think about it. But my worst loss was the death of my sister Enid, who had contracted a form of jaundice and died in Leeds Infirmary in 1942, only four years after my mother's death. I was much indebted to her husband, Pearson Crabtree, who had helped finance my practice and who had the daunting task of bringing up their three young children, Pat, Jennifer and Christopher, without their mother.

While thousands of servicemen and women came back to swell the dole queues, I had a business to attend to, which within days of re-opening the surgery, took off like a rocket. The problem was that we did not have the house to ourselves. In spite of a properly negotiated lease and no less than four months' warning of our intended repossession, the young Irish couple in occupation showed no inclination to look for other accommodation. The new Labour Government had legislated to give sitting private tenants security of tenure, especially where there were young children. When I pressed our unwelcome guests, a child of very tender years was miraculously produced. The fact that this couple had spent the war at Hawker's Aero factory at Kingston, earning better money than I was getting in the RAF, did nothing to soothe my feeling of injustice.

We had no choice but to make the best of it. I had plans drawn up to convert a small bedroom into a kitchen, install a downstairs lavatory, and let the family live upstairs, leaving us with the ground floor. I put everything into the hands of a builder and awaited the results while attending to an increasing number of patients.

The weeks passed and I slowly lost patience. After some months without result I went to see a plumber I knew from my pre-RAF days, who explained the system. Builders had to get permits for materials, available only from one of the 'quangos' the Labour Government had set up. Without permits, no builder would risk being struck off the approved list by starting work prematurely. Could anything be done? It certainly could. The plumber was a man of action, and offered to do all the work involved and to start immediately.

Within a week, working late into the night, the alterations were all complete and satisfactory.

The next upheaval came with the winter quarter's gas bill. We had agreed with our tenants that as gas fires were the only means of heating the upstairs rooms, we would pay all bills. We were not prepared, however, for the one that came through the letterbox one day. The rent had been frozen at 30/- per week, but the gas bill came to the equivalent of two years' rent!

Needless to say, I lost my temper, and instructed my solicitor to take the matter to court. He wrote to the couple accordingly, and about a week after his letter they simply disappeared. At last the house was ours, though financially we had got the rough end of the stick.

Meantime the Government were determined to implement one of the central features of their Manifesto - free medical treatment for all. Proposals detailing the intended workings of the National Health Service were circulated to all medical and dental practitioners and created a furore in those professions. The bulk of opinion, among whom I numbered myself, was bitterly opposed to it, and not without good reason. Among major causes of concern were the piece-work payment system to dentists, the recruitment of poorly qualified practitioners into the service, and the rule of bureaucracy.

It became increasingly obvious to the Labour Government and Aneurin Bevan (Minister for Health) that unless he could cajole, bribe or blackmail, he could not launch his scheme without the co-operation of the linchpins - the doctors. Dentists were only dragged in because giving away false teeth and all the rest of the dreaded dentists' stock-in-trade could prove a vote-catcher. Both professions set up fighting groups, and I from the outset could see that this scheme, politically-based and not properly thought through, could do little other than lower the standard of both professions - which then stood amongst the best in the world. In fact the British Medical Association was to international Medicine what the M.C.C. is to Cricket and Wimbledon is to Tennis. It had always been the practice of the B.M.A. and B.D.A. (British Dental Association) not to recognise most foreign qualifications. The B.M.A.'s list of non-approved qualifications was even more comprehensive than that of the B.D.A. The reason of course was that these foreign gentlemen were trained to a standard well below that of the British, with a number quite unable either to write or speak English. Communication between doctor and patient or chemist or even between British doctors of different ethnic origin would therefore be fraught with the likelihood of misunderstanding.

Then the Labour Government came up with their wonderfully simple answer. Legislate for any foreign qualified doctor or dentist to practise in Britain and jobs would be created for them under the N.H.S., irrespective of the views of the B.M.A. or B.D.A. In other words to pull the carpet from under our feet.

However, what really motivated the opposition of these two august bodies was not their inbuilt conservatism but the realisation that the high standard of British medicine and dentistry would be eroded, as the country would be swamped with get-rich-quick dentists and doctors. The gullible British public would neither know nor care what kind of treatment they were being subjected to, so long as they got it for nothing.

To fight the introduction of the N.H.S., the dental profession formed Area Groups. My group extended from Hampton Court and Teddington, across to Epsom, taking in Kingston and Surbiton, Merton, Worcester Park, Cobham and Esher, etc., comprising some 175 dental practitioners. I was the Group Secretary and held office until the groups were disbanded.

As secretary I found, amongst other things, that several dental practitioners had apparently been unable to make a living at dentistry, and had therefore followed other ways of earning money. Two were taxi-drivers, another ran a restaurant. However, finding that with the introduction of this State-run Health Service, they would be handed a practice on a plate, they decided to sign on and become dental practitioners once more. Where before the N.H.S. they had been unable to attract patients to their surgeries, now with the State paying the fees, they were as busy as bees. To the public, any dentist would do so long as he came free.

In this self-evident truth lay my objection to the egalitarian Health Service; that by its system of payment, with no incentive or betterment factor, the standard could do nothing but degenerate. If one is paid the same for shoddy work as for good, then it is human nature to cut the corners on occasion and complete three indifferent jobs, instead of one properly performed. Good, sound dentistry cannot be rushed.

In my capacity of Secretary, it was necessary for me to attend at regular intervals the Central London Committee set up by the Ministry to negotiate with them over the format of the service, and their meetings were often attended by Nye Bevan and medical representatives. At one meeting, an off-the-record question was put to Bevan: "Would not the recruitment of those with poor medical qualifications lower our standards?"

I heard Bevan reply, "We must get all the doctors and dentists we can if this scheme is to be successful in satisfying the demands made upon it and what these gentlemen don't know they must learn at the expense of the British public, who can hardly complain as it's costing them nothing."

So the stage was set to lower massively the standards of medicine and dentistry. Furthermore, the teaching schools, colleges and hospitals were all told to cut drastically their courses of learning, or to compress them so that twice as many graduates were churned out. To compound my own situation further, I was elected a founder member of the Surrey Local Dental Committee and remained so for fourteen years.

With about five weeks remaining to the supposed start of the N.H.S., and the bulk of the two professions still indicating their non-co-operation, Bevan arranged to see the principals of the College of Physicians, the Royal College of Surgeons and other eminent personages. The result was a sudden change of view about the N.H.S. from on high. Three weeks before the vital day, a dental scale of fees was announced. In many cases these were double the fees dentists were on average obtaining from their patients. At the same time it was made clear that if we did not sign on the dotted line by the prescribed date, our pension rights could be affected.

After the scheme was launched, with most of the medical and

dental professions safely toeing the line, it became known that some of the leading lights in medical circles had been knighted - and the secretary of the B.D.A. had been appointed to a top dental ministry job.

The N.H.S. duly started without the 175 dentists in my group. In retrospect, it was a hopeless struggle, but I and my colleagues had been trained to a standard that was worth fighting to maintain. Attendance at my surgery continued to support my stand, at least for the time being, and some noteworthy cases came my way, though not without the occasional setback. One day, the surgery almost went up in flames. My wife, who was my only helper and performed the roles of receptionist/dental-nurse/secretary, was preoccupied at the desk at the rear of the surgery, when the patient I had been treating piped up "Excuse me, Mr. Witherwick, but I think the surgery is on fire."

I turned to find that the drawn curtains over the window next to the Ascot water heater that supplied the wash basin, had caught alight and were blazing merrily. I immediately ripped them off, threw the fiery mass on to the floor, and stamped on it until the fire was out. It was a near thing.

This window, which had frosted glass and looked out on to the street, featured in two other unlooked-for incidents. One summer's day, when the window was slightly open to assist the cooling fan, a very grimy hand released the catch and I found myself confronted by two white eyeballs staring from an almost totally black face. "Do you want your chimneys swept, Mister?" it demanded.

At that moment I was peering inside my patient's mouth, but could not stop myself from bursting out laughing. "What, now?" I answered. "In the middle of summer? We only have gas fires in here anyway."

"Sorry, mister," said the face. "I'd better get on now." Both hands and face disappeared.

Then one evening of another summer, around 5.30 when I was very busy, a face looked in through the opened casement with a more serious purpose. "Excuse me, doctor, I've a passenger in my car who is dying. Can you come quickly."

I rushed outside to the street to see what could be done. The man in the front seat of the car was certainly in poor shape. On examination there appeared to be no respiration and having ripped his shirt away I could detect no heart beat with my ear to his naked chest. I ran to the surgery, and with the help of my nurse we manoeuvred my

100

Walton gas machine alongside the car, put the face-piece over the man's nose and mouth, and turned on the oxygen full blast. While the nurse held it in position I pressed his chest in and out, but to no avail. After several minutes of hectic endeavour I gave up and directed the driver to the nearest doctor's surgery while my nurse telephoned to alert the doctor. The car drove off, but the doctor's telephone remained unanswered. I never knew the outcome of this emergency, but I suspect that the man was beyond anybody's help.

This brief period between resuming my practice after World War II and being dragooned into a Health Service I came to despise was a golden heyday. And speaking of gold reminds me of the only time I was ever asked to supply a gold denture. One day in 1947 a scruffy middle-aged man presented himself for treatment. With down-at-heel shoes, a dirty and unkempt appearance, he could well have passed for the tramp I supposed him to be. I tried to hide my amazement when he told me that the full upper denture I had recommended was to be made completely of gold.

I pointed out that this would cost a great deal, and that I couldn't even give him an estimate until I had ascertained exactly how much gold was to be used. "Never mind," he said. "Go ahead and make it."

Without so much as a deposit, or even an address, I took him at his word and put the work in hand. The denture was made, fitted, and turned out to be highly satisfactory. When he was ready to leave, with the denture comfortably in his mouth, I told him the cost. Without batting an eyelid, he produced an immaculate cheque-book, placed it on my desk, and said, "Please will you fill in the details?"

I did so and gave him the cheque to sign, which he did with a cross X thus.

He turned out to be the owner of a very large local scrap yard, and subsequently sent his many relatives and friends to me. Which only goes to show that instinct is sometimes a better guide to people than appearances may suggest. Patients are entitled to receive from their dentist the same degree of trust that they are reposing in him, and only very rarely did I have cause to regret this working principle.

Another principle I observed was to keep to my stated fees for rich and poor alike, not subscribing to the practice widespread among doctors of scaling charges to suit their assessment of the patient's means. This sometimes had unforeseen results, as when one of my patients, personal secretary to a prominent local figure, introduced their very well-to-do employer, and made the appointment for him.

On arrival he requested a complete overhaul of his dentition, which I found would include a new partial denture. This he wanted made in stainless steel, then very much in vogue.

"Now," he said, after my examination. "I am a businessman. Before you commence treatment, I would prefer you to sit down and give me an estimate of the likely cost."

While he sat in the dental chair I worked out the cost at my desk and told him.

He turned to face me, "What did you say?"

I repeated the figure, thinking from his tone that he considered it too high.

"That's what I thought you said," he replied. "But you must have made a mistake."

"No," I assured him. "That's my fee."

He rose and made for the door. "I'm sorry Mr. Witherwick," he said. "I cannot undertake your treatment. At such a low fee, your work cannot be worth having. Good day."

Doubtless I would have fared better had I been able to tailor my bill to suit my patient. I had a tempting offer from a colleague in Wimpole Street, the Harley Street of Dentistry. This man wished me to share his practice, but I had reservations. I discovered that his work was not of the very best, which it ought to have been to match his fees. Also I could not see myself charging patients of my own practice say, £1 for specific treatment, then going up to Wimpole Street in the afternoon and charging a different patient £4 for exactly the same treatment. I had only one standard, which was the best I could do, and I feared that my colleague's more variable work could rub off on me. So I never got to Wimpole Street.

At the other end of the scale was the man who in the very early (1939) and impecunious days of the practice rang my bell at about 9 p.m., asking whether I would take out a tooth for him. I said I would be glad to do so.

"What will you charge?" he demanded.

"Two and sixpence."

"But I've only got a shilling."

"Sorry," I said. "My fee is 2/6d."

"I can't pay that much."

I suddenly hit upon a way to help him. "Tell you what," I offered. "If you give me your address, and come back in a week's time to pay, I'll take your tooth out now."

He looked at me long and hard. "No, thanks," he said. "I'll go on to Woolwich. There's a dentist there who'll take it out for a shilling."

With that he went off, leaving me open-mouthed.

When I returned to the sitting-room, my wife asked me what it was all about and I told her.

"George," she reprimanded me, "we could have done with that shilling. Do you realise that all we have ourselves is 5/- to see us over the weekend?"

In that brief post-war period before the introduction of the N.H.S., I was doing quite a lot of orthodontics, mostly of a kind to level out the front teeth. These irregularities are largely due either to the narrowing of the maxilla (upper jaw) or else to the delayed eruption of the canine tooth in the human dentition, and very resistant to being pushed around!

My most interesting case concerned a young girl, aged about thirteen when her parents brought her to see me. She had no canine tooth on the left side of her upper jaw, and as the right-hand one was already in position, her smile looked somewhat off. It was this that concerned the girl's mother as well as the child herself.

An X-ray showed what I suspected. The canine tooth was unerupted, but lying at about sixty-five degrees with its head over the root of the upper left central tooth, and across the root of the small lateral tooth. There was no space for the canine anyway as the first pre-molar was hard up against the lateral tooth. Could I do anything about this seemingly impossible situation?

I remember discussing the case with my friend and colleague John McConville, who was very dubious. To move a canine through so much bone needed a massive amount of traction and a great pressure maintained for a long period, which could result in the pathological death of the tooth. Not only had the tooth to be pulled laterally through thick bone, it also had to be pulled down. However, our main disquiet was the time factor in relation to the hardening of the bone of the patient's jaw. At thirteen and a half it would take approximately one year to pull the tooth into its proper vertical position, so the girl would then be fourteen and a half. Pulling the tooth down about three quarters of an inch, into its natural and correct position, after having extracted the first pre-molar to make this possible, would occupy about nine months more, by which time my patient's jawbone would be almost at its hardest.

With the odds stacked against me I decided to have a go, since if nothing was tried then, no subsequent attempt had any hope of success.

My first fixed appliance to apply traction failed, after three months, to move the tooth one little bit. Another, much stronger appliance was made with the traction point set higher in the bone of the maxilla, and this proved successful, with a steady movement of the tooth. However, this second appliance proved my undoing in a way I had not foreseen.

The girl was by now nicely over fiteen and I had achieved the slow steady uphill traction of bringing this unerupted canine tooth into the position I had planned for it. The patient was due for her next appointment, when the first premolar was to be extracted and a new appliance fitted to commence the pulling down of the canine into the space thus created.

I was all ready for the last lap of this, my most intricate orthodontic case, when the father of the girl phoned the surgery to say his daughter would not be keeping the next appointment and wished to discontinue the treatment. I phoned the family later that day and arranged to call to see them in the evening.

The cause of the trouble was that the girl's boy-friend, aged seventeen, had issued a kind of ultimatum, to the effect that unless she gave up wearing this appliance over her teeth, he would not go out with her any more. The girl had told her parents and they had decided to cancel any further treatment. The girl later attended the surgery when I removed the appliance.

Some twelve months later I enquired if there was any sign of the canine erupting, but neither then nor the following year brought forth any sign. This is to be expected where a tooth fails to erupt at its normal time (in this case at eleven years old), and the urge to erupt is lost. Nobody has so far identified the stimulus which prompts a permanent tooth to erupt at regular known times.

Nowadays dental mechanics have devised far smaller and neater appliances to do what I was doing then. These are often made of clear plastic material, and do not cause nearly as much concern to those having to wear them as was once the case.

Chapter 9

NATIONALISATION

Following the nationwide launch of the N.H.S., the pressure on my group to join the service began in earnest. With the Government's intractable attitude towards us, we could foresee a gradual decline in the volume of work we would be able to attract. And so, in 1948, we bowed to the principle "if you can't beat them, join them," and agreed to accept patients under the Health Service on the terms proposed.

Almost immediately, my surgery became a madhouse. It was like trying to corral a herd of hungry steers, and the steps I took to control the stampede seemed only to increase the pressure and make it more demanding in its needs. At any time of the day or evening, including weekends, they would knock on the window, the door, and even let themselves in. Within two months we were working from 9.00 a.m. until 9.00 p.m. and used to finish on my Saturday half day at 4.30 if lucky. Sunday morning was mostly spent in dealing with those who were, as they said, "in terrible pain, mister." We thought that by working to quarter hour appointments we could stem the tide, but the relief proved to be only temporary.

The next radical step was to turn the garage into a second surgery, all completed over one weekend with the aid of my plumber friend Mr. Pizzey. This move really did ease the pressure, at least on myself, since it enabled me to sort out those cases which required less concentrated attention and were being treated at a slower speed, whilst another was receiving treatment. It also enabled a patient to be given an injection, to be removed to the waiting room while it took effect, and another to be brought in to the vacated chair while I was busy in the other surgery. In other words, I was spreading my one pair of hands as widely as possible into as many mouths as time permitted.

TIME was of the essence, since payment, i.e. my sole income, was directly related to piece-work which had to be completed. Many medical practitioners, paid a fixed sum for however many patients they signed on to their panel, were as busy as I was. But here the similarity ended. If they were unable to work from some stress-related or other illness, their income went on. If they were unable to shift their work-load to another partner in the practice, in came a locum. Dentists had to carry out a minimum amount of agreed work merely to pay their surgery overheads. The N.H.S. was an unforgiving taskmaster.

It was somewhere about the ninth month of this dental fandango that I saw the light - just in time I think to save my sanity. In 1947 my wife and I had managed comfortably to run the practice. Less than two years later, it took three nurses and myself all our time between the two surgeries to treat the seemingly endless stream of patients. Something, somewhere, had to give under the strain.

It was about 8.45 p.m. on this day and the last patient had gone. My nurse was trying to pick up and sort out the 'yellow perils', the name generally given to the D.E.B. forms that all patients had to sign and which we had to complete as a record of treatment undertaken and priced, all taken from the patient's record card which I filled in. (I later devised a quicker method.) Looking at the finished dentures on the bench I noticed one name on an otherwise empty card. The name recalled a difficult case which had worried me and yet I had seen him and fitted his dentures. No trouble, no adjustments. So why was that other set I had dealt with such an awful fit; nothing right about them at all? "Oh, my God" I exclaimed, dashing into the other surgery, "Miss Wignall, there's been an awful mistake! I'm sure I've fitted the wrong set of teeth to Mr. Whipcord, and Mr. What's-his-name has got them instead. I can't go on like this. If I don't know what I'm doing, this job's bigger than I can cope with."

I phoned my mechanic, Ted Macro, at Surbiton. It had now gone nine o'clock and I told him of what I had done.

"Well, Mr. Witherwick, I can't say I'm surprised," was his comment. "If you saw my workshop tonight you'd wonder how we managed to get it all done without a big muddle at this end. I'm climbing up the wall every night and dead on my feet."

"Right," I said, "I've got the answer. We're both killing ourselves for this blasted Health Scheme. What I'm going to do is to find somewhere else to live, right away from the surgery, and we'll finish

106

at, say, 6.30 p.m. and start at 9.45. Forget Saturday surgery. That'll cut your work-load and mine before we both go crazy."

My wife almost jumped for joy when I told her my plan that night, but it took us four months to find the sort of house and garden I sought and we must have looked at dozens of possible places. It had to be somewhere out of my surgery telephone directory area so that my patients would not know where to 'phone to get at me after surgery hours, otherwise I would not gain the respite and relaxation away from it all to enable me to carry on and be fit to do my job properly.

We moved out to just south of the Hog's Back, near Farnham. It turned out to be the best thing I could possibly have done, and it also gave me an opportunity to create a garden of consequence from scratch - something I had wanted to do ever since my father gave me as a child my own patch of soil to cultivate.

It was probably about this time that a certain well-known entertainer was recommended to me. I found that he needed his remaining upper teeth removed, and I fitted an "instant" upper denture. A few days later in surgery my nurse interrupted to whisper this man's name in my ear. "He's on the phone. It's urgent."

Apparently at rehearsal that morning for a TV show that was going out 'live' in the evening, his denture had fallen out. I asked him to come straight to the surgery, and then rang Ted Macro to stand by to have his wife call at my surgery to collect the new impressions. Having taken these, I discussed with Ted the procedure for making the special temporary denture I knew was required, and he worked hard to get it ready for 5.00 p.m. that day. Fifteen minutes later I fitted them satisfactorily, and guided the patient into my garage. "Now," I said, "go over some of your lines, and really shout them out."

He gave his new denture a gruelling and noisy test and off he went, full of confidence. I watched his show at 8.30 that evening, peering into the 'box' to note any sign of trouble, but all was well. The teeth stayed in place, and my famous patient and I could each relax again.

Not every undertaking in the highly skilled practice of denture-making goes so well. Prior to the N.H.S. I treated an Australian, over here for the 1948 Olympics. My wife and I had made an early start to drive out to a stretch of road between Dorking and Petersfield, where we saw the Olympic torch-bearer go past on his way to Wembley. Later that same day, this Australian, whose full dentures I had already made minor and to my mind, unnecessary adjustments to in the ten days since fitting them, turned up again in the surgery.

The man was one of those whining people who seem to enjoy complaining for the sake of it. Examination revealed no problem, but nonetheless I took the offending dentures into the second surgery on the pretext of adjusting them. In due course I brought them back and re-fitted them. "How do they feel now?" I asked him, knowing that I had done nothing to them.

He closed his mouth on them several times. "Much better now," he replied, "but I'm not happy about this...."

Before he knew what was happening, I had opened his mouth, removed the dentures and taken them them to my desk, where I wrote a cheque, returning with it to my Aussie patient. "As you are dissatisfied with the dentures, I'm going to keep them," I told him. "Here is a cheque to their cost. Good day to you."

The man was flabbergasted. He was not really complaining, he said, it was just one or two little things, etc., etc. Please could he have his dentures back and tear up my cheque, and there'd be no hard feelings. But I was satisfied that if I did so he would be more trouble that the £20 I would save on the dentures, which of course I could not recoup. I was glad to see the last of him.

Another case concerning Australians was undertaken within the N.H.S. These two, man and wife, presented themselves at my surgery. The husband wished me to make him a complete set of dentures, but what annoyed me was his attitude. "We have just come over from Australia to see a bit of this old country," he announced. "We are going on to look at the U.S.A., so when we come back from there in three weeks perhaps you will have these dentures ready."

I procrastinated to the best of my ability but was unable to persuade this obnoxious patient from treatment, since he had already signed the 'yellow peril' form. However, after he had eventually got his dentures (at my convenience and not his) he, sitting in my dental chair, took out of his jacket pocket four complete sets of full uppper and lower dentures and placed them on the instrument tray. "All this lot have been made by dentists in Australia," he said "but none of them are anything like as good as those in my mouth that you have charged me £5 for. These useless, ill-fitting dentures cost me nearly £200 back there. Why the hell don't you come down under? A clever dentist like you could make a bloody fortune."

A nice back-handed compliment from an unexpected quarter.

One day I received a telephone message from Willie Eardley-

Wilmot, whom I had met while at RAF Chipping Warden, asking for an appointment not only for himself but for his sister, who was living at Wimbledon with a very famous person in the theatrical world. I became a close friend of Willie who was one of the nicest men I have ever met, and it was a sad day for both my wife and me when his life ended in the King Edward Hospital, Midhurst; a fine example of what an Englishman should be. But his sister, Miss Wilmot, was indeed a hard nut to crack; a nice little woman, somewhat addicted to the bottle, but scared stiff of having her teeth attended to. I could hardly blame her when I clapped eyes inside her mouth.

There were no teeth standing at all, just a mass, upper and lower, of roots, many buried and decayed out of sight below gum level and some of them suppurating. I don't think I had ever seen anything like it, not even at Edinburgh Dental Hospital where we treated so many from the Grassmarket area of Auld Reekie, probably the least salubrious part of the city in the mid thirties. It seemed that it would have to be a local anaesthetic if I was to get all this buried treasure out of her mouth and yet be able to see what I was doing without having to work in a sea of blood, mostly in the dark.

But Miss Wilmot had other ideas. She did not turn up for her appointment; due apologies were made and we re-appointed her. Again she failed to appear but I was warned on the morning of her appointment. The 'phone rang; consternation from Wimbledon - her bed had not been slept in! And she had not gone to stay in her club. Nobody knew what had happened to this eccentric person, an accomplished artist and composer, whose name had been made with 'My Little Grey Home in the West'. I later learned that her eccentricity had taken her from Waterloo to a little hotel in Brighton.

My next move was to accept her excuse of being afraid of the needle and opt for a general anaesthetic. So a bed in a small hospital was booked and I contacted Dr. John Gordon, my anaesthetist, to assist me in what promised to be a tricky undertaking as all would have to be removed at one session. She would never go through it twice! However, the lady fooled me again by getting dressed late in the evening and just popping out of the hospital, hailing a taxi to Waterloo and staying the night at her club. This last escapade caused me to contact Willie and put forward my last hope. Dr. Gordon and myself would arrive, unbeknown to his sister, at her house in Wimbledon, and the friends she lived with would pop a tablet into a cup of tea to make her drowsy and half asleep when we arrived. This would enable Dr. Gordon to give her an intravenous injection (as the doctor who had come to attend to her) while I kept in the background.

This ruse worked and the deed was done on the kitchen table, with one foot on a chair and my knee on the table it was one of the most exasperating and difficult operations I had ever undertaken. Three times I went round that mouth to check that I had not missed a root, each time finding one that I had. However, to the best of my knowledge I did get them all.

She never bothered about dentures, but with the removal of the constant source of infection which was affecting her general health, she soon became a different person, looking ten years younger, I was told. Rotten teeth do no-one anything but serious harm to their general health and especially to the heart.

To put the record straight and to show how tight-fisted the N.H.S. was to the dental profession, my reward for all this endeavour, broken appointments, travelling and working under extreme difficulties was based on the number of roots extracted, and came to some £3 sterling. One could not charge for extraneous visits or travelling and Dr. Gordon took the anaesthetist's fee. If I had undertaken this case in the U.S.A. at that time my fee would have been about £250. Things may be different under the N.H.S. nowadays but in my day, for the first twenty years of this vaunted Health Service, it was as I have narrated.

The revolutionary concept of free health care for all brought into doctors' and dentists' surgeries some who were unfamiliar with either, as seemed to be the case with two male patients I treated on separate occasions. My dental chair at that time had a spittoon, attached by a movable arm to the chair. The tumbler for the mouthwash sat at the side of the spittoon. A small metal pipe with tap was the means of filling the tumbler, often done by the nurse when the patient first sat in the chair. After some preliminary work with my drill, I went to my cabinet and suggested over my shoulder that the patient wash his mouth out and spit into the spittoon. I was amazed on turning to find the patient more or less kneeling, so that he could get his mouth on to the curved end of the little metal pipe that filled the tumbler. Removing the tumbler with one hand, he had turned on the tap, filled his mouth full of water, washed it out and spat into the spittoon, still holding the glass of mouthwash placed there for the same purpose!

The other incident, while not so acrobatic, was another way of achieving the same object. I had carried out some work in this patient's mouth, and again turned away from the chair, urging him to wash his mouth out and then use the spittoon, which as usual had the tumbler of mouthwash in situ. When I looked round I was taken aback to find the patient had jumped out of the chair, taken two strides to the washbasin in the corner and had got his mouth under the cold tap which he had turned on. He then returned to the chair and spat into the spittoon, before resuming his seat.

Tactfully on both occasions the use of the tumbler of mouthwash was explained.

Certainly some folk had peculiar ideas about my profession. One day my nurse came in from the waiting room to inform me that a patient had broken his partial denture and wished to have another, there and then, whilst his was being repaired. The number of the denture which would fit was a number 7!

I was busy with a patient at the time and my reply was "Tell this chap that we don't keep a stock of partial dentures, size 7 or any other size - it's not a shoe shop. Every denture is made exactly to fit the individual's mouth, since no two mouths are the same."

My nurse returned from delivering this message. "He's going elsewhere, he says, where the dentist is more up to date than you, Mr. Witherwick."

Psychology applied to dentistry can help establish a beneficial relationship between dentist and patient. The fear experienced by most patients is a definite hindrance to their successful treatment, and has to be overcome wherever possible. I developed a number of ways to bring this about. If it was the injection they feared - and it was important to find out early on which particular part of the process triggered the panic signal - I had two answers. A waiting patient whom I had treated before could often be persuaded to talk to the first-timer about my treatment, which was invariably reassuring. Failing this, I would sit them in the dental chair, take up the syringe in front of the mirror, and proceed to inject myself. When this had taken effect, I would give my surprised patient a probe and ask him or her to stick it into my gums.

Few dared to do this, so more often than not I stuck the probe in myself. Usually patients became reassured that I was not going to hurt them, and the treatment could proceed without them jumping out of the chair whenever the needle approached their mouth.

Trust between patient and dentist is often strained when things go wrong, as they inevitably do from time to time. Once when working in one of the L.C.C. hospitals I suddenly got cramp in my right forearm and was unable to continue to extract the teeth. The anaesthetist jumped to the rescue, picked up the forceps, saying "Right, I'll finish the job, show me where they are."

They all happened to be in the left upper jaw; two pre-molars and a molar. He snapped the crowns off all three, one after the other and turned to me. "There we are. All finished!" he said proudly.

After the patient had recovered from the general anaesthetic and I had got my arm back into action, he came down to the surgery, very much in pain from the three exposed pulps of these teeth, the pulp being the main nerve box of the tooth and extremely sensitive. He was given a local anaesthetic and I removed the roots - a common enough procedure but one to be avoided where possible.

I have never forgotten my embarrassment on a particular General Anaesthetic day at the surgery. It was generally held every second Tuesday between 12.30 p.m. and 1.30 p.m. with Dr. John Gordon, a general anaesthetist to several major hospitals around Woking, Kingston and Croydon. I had cleared the mouth of teeth on the first case, a man aged about 55, and we had just finished the last case of the session when my senior nurse came into the second surgery where I was having a few words with Dr. Gordon. "Mr. Smith has just come back and says you have left one of his teeth in his mouth," she announced.

"Oh, nonsense!" I told her, visualising the inside of his mouth. "I took them all out. He must be getting his tongue on a piece of exposed alveolus. Send him off and tell him not to poke about with his tongue."

Shortly afterwards, back came my nurse, "Sorry Mr. Witherwick, but I've just looked in his mouth and there is a tooth up at the back."

With this I blew my top, not only at the patient but at my nurse for being such a B.F. as I had definitely not left any tooth in the man's mouth.

Out went the nurse, only to come back with the patient, Mr. Smith. At once I said "Sit down. Now where's this blasted toot? Open your mouth, please."

To my amazement, there it was, right at the back in his upper jaw, the crown of a wisdom tooth, sticking up about a quarter of an inch. I had to apologise and admit my mistake and offered the patient either to take it out there and then or to be given another appointment.

He was right and I was wrong but not quite as wrong as it might appear. What actually had happened, and I have never seen a similar

112

case, was that the crown of the wisdom tooth had been partly impacted on the crown of the molar in front of it, and within a very short period of time of my removing this apparently last molar, the wisdom, held down just below gum level, simply popped up. I always made it a procedure that when I had finished a case involving a clearance I ran my finger around the mouth, but even that precaution had failed here.

Once an operation is commenced, a patient is in limbo. Unforeseen complications may well prolong the ordeal by an hour or considerably more in general surgery and the pressure upon the operator, knowing he must complete, is enhanced by the worry of how, if he finds himself in fields untrodden, he can bring the operation to a successful conclusion.One such problem faced me in 1950. I was giving a mandibular injection, using a 42mm length needle, when, to my horror, the needle broke at the hub, leaving about 1½" of needle steel in the soft tissue by the ramus[1] of the mandible and nowhere in sight. The patient was quite oblivious of what had happened as I was somehow able to keep from my face, inches in front of hers, the consternation I was feeling.

I retired to allow the injection to take effect and to think.

One thing was certain. I must try now, while the broken-off needle was still in the soft tissue by the arm of the jaw. To leave it for hospital admission could result in its being halfway down the tissue of the throat. I broke out in a cold sweat, pulled myself together by sluicing my face with cold water, and went back to my patient. She trusted me implicitly and left me to "look into a little difficulty at the back of your mouth which I have discovered." I made my incision mid-way down the ramus and worked like a blind man, keeping my instruments close to the bone and holding the tissue away, but my head lamp picked up nothing - no needles in haystacks! I was getting nowhere, then I had a flash of hope. Obviously I could only find this needle by touch and what better than another metal needle of a kind that was soft and flexible - the silver needle probe? With this seldom used instrument I gently felt my way around the tissue and then came the uplifting feel of a definite contact. This needle was as slippery as an eel, so I held the silver probe against the needle with one hand and with the other I manipulated a pair of clinical tweezers. I was able to

---

[1] Ramus: this is the name given to the upright part of the lower jaw (i.e. the mandible) to form the joint into the zygomatic arch at the base of the skull.

get hold of the needle stem and with gentle upward movement the top of the needle appeared above the mass of tissue, shining in the light of my head-lamp. Changing the probe for tweezers I pulled out the broken piece of needle. Then it was a simple matter of three stitches into my initial incision and I could at last breathe a sigh of relief.

It is said that lightning never strikes twice in the same place. Well, it did with me! Another needle broke in exactly the same place within three weeks and was removed as before. The matter was taken up strongly with the suppliers, from which it transpired in a written laboratory report that owing to the recent war a percentage of a certain metal used in the hardening of this special, flexible fine steel had been reduced, and in view of my experience, all that batch of needles was being withdrawn. I'm glad to say that no breakage ever happened again.

In 1948 we made our habitual pilgrimage to Cornwall for the summer holiday and booked in at the Railway Inn, St. Agnes, hoping that we would have better luck than in the previous year. On that occasion, my prized Burberry coat, part of my demob outfit on leaving the RAF, was stolen. I had left it in a local pub, and when I went back for it, the landlord had denied seeing it. I thought I knew the culprit, but as I could not prove it, I had to accept that there were rogues even in Cornwall. When we arrived at the Railway Inn, we found things not to our liking. I visited the local GP and asked him if he could suggest a suitable alternative. Standing in his Dispensary, his trousers supported by vivid red braces, he advised me to try the farm at the far end of St. Agnes Beacon - "that is," he said, "if you don't mind sleeping in a genuine old-type gipsy caravan."

We set off in our newly acquired Morris Minor and yes, we found ourselves in a real gipsy caravan, complete with stove and bunk, and brightly painted in the genuine old style. To get down to the beach and surf at Chapel Porth, we merely walked or slid down the far end of the Beacon.

I always got out beyond where the ten-foot waves were gathering, to come in on their crushing strength. But one day I misjudged my entry into a ten-footer and it hit my back fair and square as it curled over. Down I went to eat the sand, but as I rose to the surface I knew something had happened. I had to crawl out of that massive sea as best I could on my hands and knees, because to stand was excruciating.

Shouting to my wife for assistance and to find the lost surf board, I managed in considerable agony to scramble up the Beacon to our caravan, where I lay on the floor. Any movement was sheer agony and I still had my bathing costume on.

Somewhere in the small hours of a sleepless night, having thought over my impossible plight, a plan of action developed. If the power of a curling wave could displace a disc in my back, then surely such a wave could knock it back again! The logic was alright, but could I get down into the sea?

My wife, I seem to remember, considered my idea ludicrous. However, I could see no alternative, and at least I could try. It was in fact easier to go down the Beacon on my hands and knees than to climb up it, and once in the water, its buoyancy gave me some relief from pain.

I swam out with my board beyond the breakers and picked a big 'un, but I missed the crucial part of the wave as it curled over and I was floundering around again on the sandy bottom, fortunately still gripping the board.

Swimming out again I prepared myself for the next big one, which is usually the seventh, and this time I got it right as it curled over slap in the middle of my back. Down I went, but oh, the ecstasy, as I rose to the surface! Yes, it had knocked that disc back into place and I walked out of the sea a new man.

On another occasion about then, we visited a small cove near St. Agnes, called Trevellas. it was a bit tricky getting down the road into the cove in the Morris Minor, and then we noticed a narrow road up on the right. To gain it we had to go over a little hump-backed bridge, on which sat or leaned five or six people. As we crossed, they all seemed to express consternation, one of them shouting "You can't go up there!"

I said to my wife "Did you hear that? What makes him think we can't go up here?"

After we had rounded the first bend we found ourselves on a road full of loose stones and barely wide enough to contain the car. Beyond we could clearly see that the road on the left-hand side fell sheer away, whilst on the right the hill seemed to rise almost straight up. As we followed it, the incline became so steep that even in bottom gear I could feel the rear driving wheels hard put to keep going.

Suddenly the contents of both glove pockets in the dashboard simultaneously emptied themselves into our respective laps and the car stuttered as if to stop. I could feel the sweat running down my back as I gripped the steering wheel in grim determination. Somehow we got this wonderful British car to the top and breathed a sigh of relief while I wiped the sweat off my hands and face.

When our adventure was casually mentioned in the hotel bar it caused amazement bordering on disbelief. But for the loyal testimony of my wife, nobody would have accepted that we had accidentally ascended the Blue Hills Motorcycle and Sidecar Reliability Trial Hill considered safe only for tractors and motor bikes.

Chapter 10

THE IMPERFECTIONS OF THE N.H.S.

I have never been able to call a spade anything *but* a spade, and on many occasions this habit of plain speaking has led to my undoing, as has an unwillingness to cheat in order to gain advantage. The need to "play by the rules," inculcated in me from childhood, has never left me. It was soon clear that this training would be a hindrance to my career in the Health Service, and at one memorable meeting with Aneurin Bevan, the Health Minister in the first post-war Labour Government, I gave vent to my frustrations.

I criticised the fee structure, the inefficient bureaucracy, the concept itself. As I spoke, his face grew redder and redder until I thought he would explode. His only answer was to propound the same old Socialist propaganda with which the scheme had been launched. he would not accept that standards of dentistry were being irrevocably lowered, and when he wrote down carefully my name and surgery address, I knew I had made a powerful enemy.

From then on I was especially careful to do everything by the book. Where some of my colleagues would treat a patient privately, I stuck to the letter of my contract and politely declined to do so. It proved a wise precaution. Not long after my contretemps with Nye Bevan two men, ostensibly members of the public, requested treatment outside the NHS and did their best to persuade me to accept them as patients. I sent those impostors on their way, but that was not the end ot it. A few weeks later, two different men arrived on the same errand, and received similar treatment.

In those unsettling days, before I had learned to live with the unjustices of the system I had been shanghaied into, I encountered an example of something I thought only happened in less enlightened countries than ours. My old car, that had taken me across the length and breadth of the country while in the RAF, now needed attention. All parts for civilian vehicles were still in short supply, but two garages and the AA had certified to the authorities on my behalf that a new Hardy-Spicer coupling was required for the transmission.

Eventually two official-looking men arrived to discuss this important matter. They explained that my request for the new part did not have a high priority, as patients came to me and I rarely needed to travel to them. However, they did appreciate my need for a car, and if I could see my way clear to produce a five pound note, they could make a favourable report.....

At this blatant invitation to grease their palms, I blew up. "If they pay you so little at Uxbridge that you have to spend half a day trying to scrounge a fiver from a busy dentist, then it's time you asked for an increase. This conversation will have been overheard by my staff in the surgery through that open door, and I intend to report it to the responsible Minister. You can see yourselves out."

Whether by coincidence or as the result of this episode, the Hardy-Spicer coupling arrived at my local garage five days later.

The philosophy of "grab what you can" was not confined to the distribution of goods in short supply. It was rife throughout the Health Service, as I knew from my position of secretary to professional groups, where I was privy to a number of cases where a dentist had claimed for more work than was apparently carried out on the patient. These incidents were reported to the authorities in the expectation that the individuals concerned would be called to account, but so far as I know, no action was ever taken. The waste of taxpayers' money flourished unchecked, and in my own surgery a colleague tried to convince me that by failing to claim several extra items on patients' treatment forms I was losing 10/- to 15/- per patient - a significant figure in those days.

"But that work has not been done," I pointed out.

"Well, it's there for the asking. If you don't take it, others will. You're a bloody fool to let it go."

Honest fool that I am, my response was that I would rather be able to live with my conscience and look the world straight in the face.

Personal initiative was discouraged by the standardisation that was built into the NHS from the beginning. The love of dentistry that had led me in 1942 to begin the study of 're-plantation of teeth', took a severe knock when, after many letters to and from the Dental Estimates Board in Eastbourne, I was advised that such work could not be rewarded. In 1949 I gave a clinical demonstration of what I had achieved in this new field, and if I had been able to obtain the antibiotics soon to be discovered by Professor Fleming and developed by others, I could have overcome the biggest single problem my work had encountered. Pursuing the work in secret would have involved my patients in deception and discovery would have threatened my livelihood. Reluctantly I ceased work on that fascinating project.

Another bone of contention concerned a patient with a dental condition that proved almost impossible to cure, but who had implored me to keep trying. Lengthy correspondence with the D.E.B., seeking payment for the 23 visits or appointments involved, met with an uncompromising refusal to meet my claims. This unjust decision was followed by a typical muddle with another case of husband and wife both needing full dentures, where the D.E.B. approved one but not the other. The fact that it was the wife who had filled in both forms in my waiting room did not exonerate the Board who had confused the NHS number with the National Insurance number. I begged them to write to the wife (who blamed me) and admit to their error. They would not do so, and I lost the patients and the work.

It was the culmination of these incidents that ate into my soul and caused a radical reappraisal of my place in Health Service dentistry. Wouldn't I have done better to stay in the RAF? Only a handful of dentists had attained the rank of Squadron Leader, as was confirmed by my immediate chief at Hounslow, where I had been received like a V.I.P. just prior to demobilisation. Very high rank, it was intimated, was there for the asking if I stayed on, and when no less a person than the Director-General of the RAF Dental Branch telephoned to add his voice to others, it was very difficult to resist their blandishments. My wife's preference for a home of her own had won the day, but neither she nor I had foreseen the disgruntlement that the NHS would bring about in me.

Among options I began considering was a move to the Channel Islands, where we actually looked at a practice but could not justify the cost. Then there was New Zealand, a country of great opportunity, with only one thing against it; Audrey did not want to live there.

In the end it was the move to Runfold near Farnham that saved the day. It entailed a round trip to the surgery and back of sixty miles daily, along the busy Portsmouth Road in the trusty Morris Minor I had recently acquired, and I used to allow an hour each way, arriving home around 7.45 p.m. to a hot meal followed by a couple of hours relaxing in an armchair before turning in.

Weekends were a joy. Weather permitting, I spent every spare moment in the garden. The house we had chosen, and where we were to remain for the next thirty years, was delightfully situated in four acres of natural woodland on greensand and yet had the civilised facility of two bus services passing the gates. The four-bedroomed house, designed by a Mr. Falkener of Farnham, had been solidly built by a highly reputable firm of local builders in 1919 and enjoyed splendid views from every window. Here was the haven I needed to pursue my hobbies of wood-turning and gardening, and to instigate a "grand design" of tree-planting that eventually produced a mini-Wisley of rare trees and shrubs, expecially my favourite rhododendrons and azaleas.

All this had to be paid for in terms of the stress associated with the sheer pressure of dental work, which together with the committee work inseparable from being secretary to my local dental association, sometimes brought me to the point of exhaustion. One of the more unpleasant experiences came about from treating somebody I regarded as above reproach.

The origins went back to our house in Eltham, where most weeks we would entertain a friend of my wife's and her husband, or be invited to their house. Some of our furniture was too big for our tiny place and a temporary exchange was made for certain smaller pieces of the friends' furniture, on the understanding that if we moved to a larger house, we would return their furniture and take our own with us. Two years later came our move to Runfold. My wife made it clear that we would need our pieces returned, but for some reason these friends were upset about it, and the atmosphere between us became rather cool.

I had already taken out the woman's teeth and made dentures that she was very pleased with, all under the NHS. Now she decided she wanted another set made.

She and her husband had acquired through our close friendship quite a detailed knowledge of the rules and regulations governing my practice, and were well aware of how to use the complaints procedure to inflict maximum embarrassment or even damage to my reputation.

I was amazed to be called before the Final Complaints Committee to answer charges of unprofessional conduct, and horrified when, in answer to one of those questioning her, she implied in an aside that sexual intimacy took place in my surgery.

The presiding Chairman, who took it very seriously, wrote a note which was passed to me. "Did you or did you not seduce this patient?" it read.

"Certainly not," was my signed answer.

The woman was then asked to detail the reasons for her complaint. I listened with dismay and anger at the tirade of vindictiveness that spilled out so glibly that she must have rehearsed it night after night. Her main point was that the extra money she claimed to have paid me had in no way improved on the original dentures, though it was obvious to me that they had altered her appearance greatly for the better. She further claimed that our "arrangement" had been made in the privacy of my surgery, with nobody else present.

My nurse, the only witness I could call, now intervened dramatically. A slight, trim little figure, whom I had seen as more mouse than virago, she rose and banged the table with her hand. "That woman is a wicked liar!" she cried in a shrill, piercing voice, white-faced with emotion.

A stunned silence greeted this bombshell. When the effect of it had sunk in and she was asked to resume, she gave a precise account of events that was listened to intently by the Committee. It was her fundamental duty, she told them, never to absent herself from the surgery when the surgeon was treating a woman patient. She had never left it during any of the woman's several appointments, and at no time had that patient discussed paying extra for her dentures, and the suggestion of any intimacy was ridiculous. The whole complaint was a tissue of lies from beginning to end.

Under questioning she did not waver, and her testimony clearly convinced the Committee of her honesty. Meanwhile the complainant completely lost her composure and sobbed bitterly on her husband's shoulder.

"Do you have anything further to say?" I was asked.

"Well, Mr. Chairman," I replied, "I had intended to say quite a lot, but I cannot think of anything that would prove my innocence of these charges more effectively than the spontaneous testimony you have just heard from my nurse."

The Chairman then declared the meeting closed, and before I left the building I had the satisfaction of being told by the Clerk that the case against me was not proven.

After this I was very wary about giving dental treatment to friends. They, after all, were the ones who expected me to work after hours for them; would turn up late for appointments and wreck my already tight schedules; who called me 'George' in the hearing of my patients, to whom I maintained a strictly professional manner. My insistence on a nurse being present at all times in the surgery did not, however, help me in the matter of Mrs. X, a plump, attractive woman who became my patient, and after treatment one day spun me a tale about her husband, a clerk, being unable to pick her up from the surgery as his car had broken down and was under repair.

Gallantry overcame caution when I volunteered to drop her at her house in Esher on my way home. When we arrived, she persuaded me to have a drink while she excused herself to go upstairs to change. A few minutes passed before she appeared on the staircase, and changed she certainly was! Through her open dressing-gown I could see she was stark naked!

How things might have gone after that is anybody's guess. It's far from easy for a man to spurn such an obvious advance, but at that moment the husband came in, his car having presumably received some miraculous mechanical cure. Five minutes later and I would have been sitting with his wife on the lounge sofa, and who would have believed my version in any trumped-up complaint? Woman can be so devious, and a white coat is no protection. In some ways it leaves one more vulnerable.

As though to redress the balance, it was a middle-aged woman patient who became the innocent victim of my worst mistake. She had presented herself with advanced gum trouble necessitating major gum resection in gingivectomy, which for some obscure reason I carried out within my second surgery, and this subsequently proved the major cause of all the suffering inadvertently inflicted upon this patient. Having carried out the gingivectomy, I reached over to my instrument cabinet and took a medicament bottle from the line of bottles, all named, but all of the same size and pattern. Assuming it was the Absolute Alcohol I intended to use, I took a small wad of cotton wool with my tweezers and swabbed the entire operational area with it before dismissing the patient and making a further appointment to renew the soothing dressing around the necks of the teeth.

I was taken by surprise the following morning to find this patient already seated in the surgery washing out her mouth with warm mouth wash provided by my nurse, and clearly in great distress, with tears running down her face. "Oh, Mr. Witherwick, what has happened?" she cried. "My teeth are all on fire."

I was dumbfounded. What did she mean? How could those lower front teeth be so painful? Infection there certainly had been, but nothing to cause this state of affairs. Besides, the pain seemed to be dispersed all along the six front teeth and the epithelium of the gum, labially and on the tongue side very inflamed. What on earth had caused this sudden outbreak of infection, that at the time seemed to me the only possible cause of such pain?

I did what I could to give her comfort with a soothing dressing and set up another appointment.

The next day the picture was sadly much worse and so was the poor woman. The gum tissue around the lower front teeth was now blanched, almost devoid of blood, hard and dry, and the pain seemed to the patient to be eating into the jaw bone itself. Another type of dressing was applied and she was sent home.

Her next visit was on the Monday morning, and by now the situation looked horrifying. Not only had the skin around the teeth sloughed off, but the surface of the exposed bone was blackish in colour. Even worse - and this really shook me - I could elicit no pain reaction to my probe from any point around the six lower teeth. The whole area was dead tissue, though the pain had abated somewhat.

That night, lying awake pondering the situation, the evidence seemed to point to an alarming mix-up. As soon as I arrived at the surgery next morning, I went straight to the medicaments, took out the Absolute Alcohol bottle and looked at its label. Phenol!! I took out the stopper and smelt it, and there could be no doubt. My long-suffering patient had good cause to feel her teeth were on fire, bathed as they were in carbolic acid!

I promptly rang up all likely sources of advice, but nobody I spoke to had experienced my predicament. So I made a paste of zinc oxide and absolute Eugenol, and to give it a degree of adhesion, mixed pure lard with it! Fortunately I had by me a small amount of some special silver-lined paper which was smeared with healing ointment of a non-irritant nature and having some degree of waterproof adhesion, which I had seen used in the theatre of the Maxillo-facial Unit at East Grinstead by that eminent surgeon, Sir John McIndoe.

Within forty eight hours, what had seemed irretrievable suddenly became healthy. I could almost see the new tissue being formed as I changed the dressing, the old dressing taking with it the dead debris and the fresh one encouraging new growth. With the pain and discomfort daily receding the patient's spirits were buoyant and her thanks profuse.

Having changed the tide of depair to one of hope, I at once carried out an investigation into the incident to make sure it could never happen again. I remembered that some few weeks prior to this happening I had been laid low with a heavy and highly infectious cold. In my absence, my nurses had used the opportunity to empty and clean the dental cabinets in both surgeries. The medicament bottles were labelled and set out strictly in alphabetical order, identical in each surgery. All the instruments were laid out in the same strict order, always in the same place in the same drawers or cupboards; a place for everything and everything in its place. Somehow in the cleaning-up process the Absolute Alcohol bottle had changed places with the Phenol bottle, both being identical clear liquids in identically shaped bottles.

The nurse in question was reduced to tears and I to exasperation, but we ensured that the mistake could never happen again. The Phenol bottle was changed for one of entirely different shape and colour and removed to another position away from the others.

The patient fortunately made a complete recovery, giving me a lesson in surgery management unlikely to be forgotten, and the nurse an indication of what can happen when attention to detail is allowed to lapse.

The fall in standards of dentistry forecast by myself and others began to show itself in various ways, not least in the scramble for business by equipment manufacturers and suppliers of materials, who sometimes put on to the market products that were inadequately researched. One such was a batch of artificial teeth of such low masticating strength that within a year of use the teeth on the dentures were virtually non-existent. Naturally the patient was soon back again, blaming me and demanding a new set. Across the country, money was pouring into dentists' pockets, swelled by the many bogus claims. Something had to be done, and eventually the Labour Government acted. It cut dentists' fees for every item of treatment by 25% and instituted charges for treatment.

There were howls of protest from the doctrinaire Left, who regarded the NHS as a bottomless well of money to be dipped into as occasion demanded. When it was clear that the Government would stand by its proposals, Aneurin Bevan announced his resignation, though making sure before he went that his pension and other rights were protected.

To the 'wide-boys' of our profession, the cut in fees made little difference. They simply fiddled the claim forms even more to allow for it. For me it was a body blow. I agonised over the accounts, looking for ways to economise. But nowhere could I find the means to cut the surgery overheads, which accounted for 52% of my gross income. There was only one thing to be done. Instead of 17 appointments daily, I would have to work 27 to bring in the same income after tax. It was a worrying prospect, but as there appeared to be no alternative, I took that course. The treadmill that we had geared ourselves to was now demanding even more effort to maintain its momentum, and for some it was too much. My own relatively small circle in Surrey, in the 20 years between 1949 and 1969, was depleted by no less than seven dentists, four of them by death, three from breakdown, all succumbing at the height of their professional lives. Perhaps it is as well that we rarely know what is in store for us.

During the fifties, my wife and I derived great pleasure in spending our holidays in Cornwall, where we later bought a charming cottage, and on travelling to other parts of the country to stroll among many of the famous gardens, such as Stourhead, Westonbirt, Bodnant, to name only a tiny proportion of those we enjoyed. As the direct result of one of those visits, I conceived the plan of planting a whole new woodland of 600 trees in a clearing I had made in the four acres of our Runfold garden, and very successful it turned out to be. But travelling always involves the risk of being in the wrong place at the wrong time, and it was in North Wales on a visit to the lovely gardens at Bodnant that we came close to disaster.

One evening after dinner at the little country hotel, we set off along a back road in our Morris 1000 saloon headed for Caernarvon. At a tee-junction we turned right and commenced a long, steep ascent along a secondary road. Ahead of us I suddenly saw a lorry coming down the hill towards us, trailing black smoke. The road was only wide enough for two vehicles and the lorry was occupying the middle of the road.

Instinctively I pulled tight into my nearside and stopped. As the lorry approached, the black smoke became denser and something big appeared to drop beneath it while I and my wife sat petrified. Now the driver put his finger on the horn button and left it there, at the same time opening the door of his cab as though about to jump, which would have been suicidal at that speed. Instead he waved his right arm frantically for us to get off the road, which of course was quite impossible as there was nowhere to go! Getting no reaction from us, he squirmed back behind the wheel, and with horn still blaring, the juggernaut roared past us with no more than three or four inches to spare and rocking the car with its proximity.

Nervously I re-started the engine, made a three-point turn in the road, and followed in the wake of the lorry, which had stopped on an incline at the next bend with its wheels in a ditch and the front through the hedge. We saw that it was loaded with bricks, the weight of which alone could have crushed us to pulp. To our amazement, the driver emerged from his cab unscathed, subjecting us to a torrent of invective for not getting out of his way. The gearbox had gone, the brakes were useless, and we were lucky to be alive.

Another incident concerning a lorry occurred in the fifties during what became known as the Great Smog which brought parts of London to a complete standstill. It was on a Friday, when I held a late surgery. I finished at 7.30, by which time the fog was very dense. The route was familiar from my weekday commuting, but the five-minute run to gain the Kingston Bypass took twenty-five. I thought I could now make better speed, but within minutes of going through the underpass at the Ace of Spades in fog so thick that ten miles an hour seemed fast, I braked hard to stop inches from the bonnet of another car. Somehow the driver had missed his turn-off for Leatherhead, and was now driving the wrong way along the underpass, against the traffic.

I had to try and help stop the traffic behind us while he turned his car in the road and I set him off with new directions. Progress resumed at no more than 10 mph until we reached the Scilly Isles at Esher, when a motor-bike and sidecar passed me. I followed his bright tail-light until it came to a sudden stop, the combination being wedged between a bollard and lamp-standard whose light was barely a glow.

"Where are we?" I asked the motor-cyclist.

"Esher, I think."

"I don't remember those bollards," I said.

Footsteps sounded and a dim figure loomed in the swirling yellow fog. "Do you know where this is ?" I called out.

"Claygate," came the answer. We were five miles north of Esher.

Between us we got my friend's combination on the road again, leaving him in Esher while I made for Cobham. There I was overtaken by a heavy lorry, and wasn't I glad to trail along behind him, close to his tailboard!

We bowled along together, much faster than I could have chanced on my own, and I was just thinking that the worst of my journey was over when I heard a terrible crash. The tailboard of the lorry seemed to rush towards me as my car collided with it and wedged itself underneath.

Shaken up but unhurt, I got out to investigate the accident. We were in an oak wood and the lorry cab had wrapped itself around one of the massive boles, trapping the driver between it and the damaged door which would not open. Through the now glassless window I could see the unconscious driver, who, when I reached through to slap his face repeatedly, became groggily conscious. Luckily his legs were free, and I was able to ease him out through the window. By this time he had recovered sufficiently to help me extricate my car, and together we tried to work out which way to go. A passing motor-cyclist helped with directions to Ripley, where I dropped the lorry-driver to telephone his firm and the police.

All went well then until, in the still dense fog, I missed the turn-off for the Hogsback and ran on to boggy ground where I promptly got stuck. Fate or foresight had ensured that in the footwells of the car were two heavy-duty rubber mats, the ribs being reinforced with metal - ideal for putting underneath the rear wheels which, with the help of a delicately-used clutch, finally gripped and got me out of another tricky situation.

The faithful Morris 1000 Traveller took me safely on until, within a stone's throw of my house in Runfold, I came upon a horse-box slap in the middle of the road. Two loose horses were milling about, but with no sign of anybody in charge. I carefully manoeuvred the car past this eerie sight, and arrived home with heartfelt thanks at 10.45 p.m., fortunate to have got there at all and to the great relief of my wife who expected the worst.

Driving to work on the Monday morning I saw the lorry, still embedded in the oak wood just past the Wisley Hut Hotel, and where it was to remain for more than a week. I paused to reflect on the fact that the driver had been on the wrong side of the road when he entered the wood. Had he veered to the left instead, we should both have ended up in the lake!

Chapter 11

DIAGNOSIS - OR IGNORANCE

The practice of dentistry, especially as intensively as I was obliged to perform it during my 20 years under the NHS, is physically very wearing, to say nothing of its effect on the surgeon's nervous system. Few people consider the strength required to extract difficult teeth, the effects on the spine of the unnaturally stooped position the dentist must adopt when examining or treating patients, and the precision and concentration required which calls for absolute steadiness of hand and perfect coordination between brain and body. I had started with an advantage. At college I was considered something of an athlete, with trophies galore. I learned to play golf to a handicap of five, and latterly enjoyed the more vigorous tasks in my various gardens. In short, I was a very fit and active man. Nonetheless, it was not long before the strain showed, and on numerous occasions I had to consult NHS doctors.

I am sorry to say that my experiences with these gentlemen were far from satisfactory. On the whole they bore out the many tales of woe related by patients in my surgery which, even allowing for exaggeration, would either constitute an indictment of NHS practice of the time or support the proposition that medicine can never be an exact science. I incline to the former view.

During 1956 my right wrist became intensely painful, and as I am right-handed, this caused me considerable apprehension. I went to see one of the doctors who had helped me with general anaesthetic cases.

This GP, after listening to what I had to say, said without any further ado, "I'm very sorry Mr. Witherwick, but from my experience I'm afraid you are suffering from arthritis in the bones of your wrist joint. I've seen any amount of cases, and I've no hesitation in making this diagnosis."

"What can be done about it?" I asked him.

"Very little, I'm sorry to say. The best treatment is a course of Golburg injections, one every fortnight, six in all. We must then hope for the best."

I was ready to jump to anything that offered hope of a cure. "When do we start?" I asked him. "What about an injection now?"

"Very well," he said.

I proceeded to expose my buttocks and received the jab, which certainly made me wince, but it was while I was dressing myself that he really hurt me -

"I have to say that there is very little hope that these injections will cure your condition. Moreover, your fingers and other joints may well become infected. My honest advice to you is to seriously think of selling your practice and take up some other kind of work."

This latter advice, to a man in his mid forties, was quite shattering. However, at the next general anaesthetic session in my surgery I confided in Dr. John Gordon, my anaesthetist, who was most concerned. That same evening he telephoned to say that he had spoken to a colleague who was a specialist in rheumatoidal and arthritic complaints, and who would be glad to offer consultation and examination if I so wished.

At my third visit to the GP for another jab, I tackled him and suggested that in view of the serious implications for my future career, would he refer me for an examination to a consultant?

The doctor became very agitated. There was absolutely no need for a second opinion. He had seen so many of these cases that there was no mistake in his diagnosis. It was just a waste of time to see anyone else. When I persisted in my request, I regret to say that the interview became most heated, ending with my saying that I intended anyway to see the consultant, whom I named.

With this I was abruptly shown out of his surgery and the door slammed behind me. I never saw the man again.

I duly presented myself to the consultant who lived, I think, in Cobham. I was subjected to a very thorough examination and later sent to Surbiton Hospital for X-rays and urine tests.

"There is positively no sign of any form of arthritis," the specialist informed me later. "Lay off all this digging in the garden for a couple of months, and the pain should gradually go."

I took his advice, and the condition cleared up, as he had forecast.

Another problem was with a stiff neck. This became so painful that it took a great effort to raise myself from the bed each morning and several aspirin to get me through the day. Finally, after sleeping in each of the five bedrooms of our house in turn and keeping the windows of my car closed to eliminate any possibility of draught being the cause, I gave in and sought advice.

An eminent professor at the Middlesex Hospital Clinic near Regent's Park heard me out before asking what I did for a living. When I confessed to being a Dental Surgeon he burst into peals of laughter that could have been heard in the Strand. "Occupational hazard!" he roared. "You chaps are always down in the mouth." More hilarious laughter.

The pain I was suffering did not allow me to share the joke. "I'm glad you think it's so funny," I said stiffly, getting off the chair and making for the door. "I suppose you'll be telling me next to give up my calling and push a barrow down the Old Kent Road selling bananas."

He was still laughing as I went out.

A few weeks later I happened to be treating a Flight Lieutenant from the RAF Rehabilitation Unit at Chessington. He was a medical man, in charge of this specialised unit. When I mentioned my difficulty he said, "From what you've told me I can probably help you. Can you come to see me tomorrow morning?"

Filled with hope, I accepted the opportunity and re-arranged my next morning's appointments. The Flight Lieutenant, whose name was Knight, quickly inspired my confidence. He was already treating a number of similar cases involving PT instructors who performed somersaults over the vaulting-horse at the Royal Tournament at Olympia each year. There was a distinct similarity between their symptoms and mine.

The treatment he recommended was to fit me with a neck-band or harness, which I was to wear every day. At night I was to discard my pillows so that my head and spine would be in the same line on the board of wood he advised me to place on the mattress and sleep on.

I did everything he said, with the happy result that within three months all pain had vanished and the condition, now known as Cervical Spondylitis, did not return. If Flight Lieutenant Knight is still alive and reads this, I hope he will accept my grateful thanks

On another occasion I consulted a GP about a swollen knee joint. As the pain had been increasing week by week to the stage where it was almost impossible to stand on it and I was losing sleep, one would have thought that a thorough clinical examination would be called for.

Not a bit of it. Without laying as much as a finger on the knee, this doctor knew all about my problem. Looking at it, he opined that I must have given the knee a knock, displacing the patella (knee-cap), and thereby increasing the synovial fluid that lubricates this and other joints of the body.

Nothing I said dissuaded the doctor from his diagnosis. I had become convinced that I was suffering from some form of arthritis in the joint, so fixed up an appointment at a clinic in Gt. Portland Street, London, where I saw a specialist by the name of Savage. He examined my knee carefully with his fingers and finally hit a point on the inside of the joint that caused me to leap out of the chair.

An X-ray followed, and when he had examined this the specialist gave his opinion. "You have rheumatoid arthritis in your knee. Unfortunately it's well established and should have been dealt with months ago. It's doubtful whether it will now respond to treatment. Your doctor must be blind."

This diagnosis was not promising. It was no comfort to know that it agreed with my own. However slight the chance of successful treatment, it was something I had to try, and the specialist agreed.

I was prepared for the pain of the injection right in the middle of the swollen knee, although I could not restrain a yelp of pain. But when I got outside and tried to walk down the street, the pain was so fierce I collapsed on the pavement. Some good Samaritan, seeing me in such distress, stopped to offer help. He hailed a taxi and helped me in, bound for Waterloo Station en route to Surbiton where I had left the car. Somehow I managed to drive back to Runfold, still in great pain.

The happy sequel was that after six weeks and three more injections, the problem with the knee simply disappeared and did not recur. I felt obliged to report the outcome to the GP who had been so convinced of his own wrong diagnosis. What did he say? "Sorry old chap. It never entered my head that it might have been rheumatoid arthritis."

Whatever else may have been in his head, it was certainly not the principles of proper clinical examination that had formed the basis of my own professional training in diagnosis.

The old adage that troubles never come singly could well have applied to my own situation in 1956. In May of that year I developed symptoms of dysentery, and despite a growing disillusionment with the NHS as regards the efficiency of some of its medical practitioners, I once again presented myself at a doctor's surgery. The Calomel I was prescribed did nothing to help, and after three weeks or so I consulted another GP whose surgery at Surbiton was close to my own. He prescribed the same ineffective treatment. By now I was having to stop three or four times to relieve myself in the course of the 30-mile journey to my practice. It was as though whatever I ate went straight through me.

Both GPs assured me that the problem lay in what I was eating, but agreed to refer me to Surbiton General Hospital, where I was subjected to X-rays, Barium Meals, and a very fine implement that lit up at the top end and looked like a submarine periscope, which was pushed up my back passage to the giggling delight of two young NHS nurses. Having dressed myself after these various indignities, I was ushered into the presence of the specialist, and the question of my diet discussed.

"A lot of folk have loose bowels as a normal feature of their lives," declared the specialist. My protestations that I, on the contrary, had spent most of my life resisting a tendency towards *constipation*, should have convinced him to think again. Instead, he leaned across the desk, informed me that all the tests showed that there was nothing wrong with me, and intimated that I was wasting his time.

After enduring seven weeks of debilitating diarrhoea while puting in a very full week at the surgery, to be seen as a malingerer by a man earning several times my income for much less effort was the last straw. I got up and walked out.

For reasons unknown to me then, the diarrhoea became less, and within a few days of returning from the specialist, it ceased. However, I noticed a loss of energy and felt tired from even moderate exertion. So without understanding what was wrong with me, I curtailed my gardening activities, rested whenever possible, and kept going through the winter of 1956/7.

Easter saw me in Cornwall with my wife, snatching two extra days from work in a bid to pull myself together and recover my habitual fitness.

On Easter Sunday, Audrey and I went to look at the now-famous garden at Caerhays owned by J.C. Williams, celebrated for the wonderful new strains of Camellia he developed. An hour later, feeling most peculiar in the lavatory, urinating felt like passing concentrated acid.

We decided to leave for our cottage at Rose, near Goonhavern, and in bed that night I felt most unwell. A severe abdominal pain woke me in the early hours which increased during the morning so that only by sitting with my knees up to my chin could I obtain any relief. Instead of having my wife call the doctor I prevailed on her to walk to the village store for Aspirin, which by the Tuesday morning I was taking at the rate of four every hour.

By now Audrey had called in a doctor from a group practice at Perranporth. He started to listen to what I had to say, then interrupted from the end of the bed. "I know what's wrong with you, old boy. Had it myself. You've got inflammation of the bladder from walking along the beach in that East wind. I'll prescribe something for you to take every four hours. It'll make you as right as a trivet and you'll be able to drive back to London in the morning."

On that optimistic note, and without taking my temperature, feeling my pulse or establishing the seat of the pain, he went out. I called down to ask him if he would give Audrey a lift to Perranporth, and when she returned with the prescription she insisted on staying up all night to ensure I had the medicine. Her faith was stronger than mine.

Just before dawn I suddenly felt better. I lay back on the pillows, exhausted.

It was wonderful to be free of the terrible pain. For an hour or two I felt excited. That young doctor knew his stuff after all. I was on the mend.

Hardly had I got used to the idea when I began to feel peculiar in a way I had not known previously. It was now impossible to pass more than a few drops of water without the intense burning sensation I had experienced at Caerhays. Audrey went to the village again to telephone for the doctor, and what she told me on her return almost destroyed my faith in human nature. According to the Practice receptionist, the doctor in question was not contactable. It was his day off. In any case, there was no record of his having attended me. Moreover, if my condition had been serious he would have entered it in the Duty Book, and there was no such entry. As the receptionist had no precise information about me, she could not call in another doctor.

Faced with this scarcely believable story, anger temporarily overcame restraint. I got out of bed and announced my intention of walking to the village in my dressing-gown. At this, my wife set off once more.

Later in the morning she returned with the news that another doctor would call sometime during the day. The waiting now became intolerable, and I was gradually losing my grip on reality. By the time the doctor arrived around 6.30 in the evening, I was talking gibberish and ranting like any dictator.

The appearance of Dr. Robb, principal of the Group Practice and a man who had qualified prior to the Health Service, eased the situation. After a detailed examination of my abdomen, probing and listening, he straightened and paced the bedroom before addressing me. "I'm afraid you're very ill," he said. "Whatever the trouble is, it's serious. I shall get a Consultant here from Truro Infirmary as soon as possible. Meantime, do not try to pass water, and lie as quiet as possible."

About three hours later he returned with a Mr. Rutter, senior consultant at the Infirmary, who asked many questions and subjected me to a further meticulous examination before withdrawing to consult with his colleague. "Your condition is acute," he said on returning. "We must get you into hospital at once so that I can operate on you tonight."

At last, after almost a year, somebody was acting responsibly. The ambulance arrived within the hour, but the poisons in my bloodstream were having a distrubing effect on my state of mind. In hospital I became obstructive and abusive, refusing to allow the Indian technician to X-ray me, to sign permission for a general anaesthetic, or to let the nurses shave my pubic and anal hair. Valuable time was wasted in calming me in readiness, and it must have been almost midnight before I was anaesthetised. Prone and mercifully silent on the trolley, my departure for the Operating Theatre was doubtless greeted with relief by all concerned.

Recovering from the two-hour operation, I was able to learn what had been happening inside me. It appeared that an abcess had formed in the diverticulum of my bowel, or alimentary canal. When it burst through the peritoneum it discharged its poison into my system, giving rise to a massive increase in toxins which quickly overwhelmed the body's purifying organs. Peritonitis, as the condition is commonly known, generally leads to the death of the patient if not operated on within twenty-four hours. By my calculations, a further five or six hours of delay in getting me to hospital would have seen me knocking at St. Peter's Gate instead.

The operation I had undergone is known as a Gastrotomy and Colostomy. It left me with a stomach stitched from navel to genitals like a hot cross bun, complete with protruding drainage tube and a little rosebud on the left-hand side for the plastic bag that for a couple of months or so was to serve as a collector of waste-products - in fact an outside privy that dissuaded one's nearest and dearest from getting too close, as there was no control over its use and no means of fumigation. Mr. Rutter came frequently to check progress and could never understand how my various medical advisors had failed to connect symptom with cause, any more that I could.

In the intensive-care ward at the end of a passage to which Matron had assigned me, I had the misfortune to be attended by a lady house surgeon, whose incompetence on one occasion drew a public reprimand from Mr. Rutter. On another, she spent over an hour with me, attended by two nurses, struggling to insert a needle into a vein in my left arm for an intravenous drip. When she gave up to try her luck with the other arm, berating me for having "such piddling little veins," the arm had swollen to the size of my thigh and was sky-blue in colour. I was forced to suffer in silence, knowing that I could have done it myself in a few seconds.

My recovery was hampered by the distinctly hostile atmosphere I sensed around me. Here I was, practising in the NHS, entitled to benefit from all available services, yet resented by those who considered that a Dental Surgeon should not be having treatment in a state-run hospital. The theme, stated or implied, went like this. "As a dentist earning thousands of pounds a year, you have no right to be taking up a bed that could be used for a poor person and preventing them from getting treatment."

This view seemed to be general among nursing and ancillary staff and the louder-voiced patients who, like good Socialists, envied all those who appeared to be in a better position than themselves. In this union-dominated environment, it was inevitable that I would find myself in conflict with the restrictive practices that characterised it.

With the gradual regaining of my strength, and release from the confines of the intensive-care ward, the sheer boredom of hospital routine (one could hardly call it 'life') was hard to bear. I looked around for something to do and hit upon the idea of barbering. This activity took me around the Male Surgical Ward every morning and passed the time very pleasantly until I encountered an interfering trolley-pusher in a white coat. He looked like one of the Hall's Distemper men one used to see displayed on advertising hoarding by railway lines in the 'thirties and voiced his disapproval of what I was doing.

"I'm going to report you," he said.

"Who the hell to?" I demanded.

"Your Union."

"We'll see about that."

I dashed off and came back with a cut-throat razor borrowed for a patient. I brandished it in his face and threatened to use it if he interfered any more. He kept out of my way after that.

Soon I was well enough to leave hospital and convalesce at our cottage. I fretted at the enforced idleness, but the main worry was centred on my practice, for which I had needed a locum in my absence. A kind friend and colleague in Surbiton had arranged for a young South African dentist to stand in for me, the NHS regulations demanding that any treatment commenced had to be finished. And here was the rub. Unlike NHS doctors, whose locums took responsibility for their own work while the doctor was away, I was responsible for my assistant's work, even though I could not supervise him from Cornwall. The financial loss bothered me too, as I earned nothing myself for four months, and stood to lose all our savings as a result.

When I received the first monthly cheque in Cornwall for my locum's efforts, I thought there must be some mistake. The amount represented more than two months' average income! I had good reason to believe that nobody could deal with more than fifty appointments daily throughout the week, which they would have had to do in order to earn such a sum. I began to have suspicions.

The following month, another cheque arrived, for a similar incredible amount. Now I knew something was wrong, especially as I was informed that the locum had taken himself off with the comment that there was now insufficient work to justify his continued engagement.

I resumed my practice at the end of August, and within a month had been able to examine some of the patients treated by the locum. It was soon apparent that the amazing amounts of money he had claimed were the fruits of his dishonest brain rather than the rewards for superhuman effort. When I compared the patients' individual record cards, it was clear that of the fillings he had claimed for -

sometimes seven or eight at a time - only one or two were his own work in each case. The others were mine, made and claimed for over the years before! I was certain the DEB at Eastbourne would soon be on my back, demanding to know how in two months I had suddenly earned the equivalent of four months' work or more.

I worried unnecessarily. Nothing happened. Maybe the abuses of the system were so widespread that the DEB turned a blind eye or else did not bother to check. Many Commonwealth-trained dentists on a two-year stay, lured to this country by the rich pickings to be found on the plump corpus of the NHS, went the rounds as assistants or locums, moving on after three or four months and before their integrity could be called into question. Nor were they any more to blame than some of my own colleagues.

The crux of it all was summed up one day in the surgery by a young fellow I had just treated. Before following the nurse to fix up another appointment he stopped to speak to me. "If you don't mind my saying so, I think you're a bloody fool," he told me.

What does one say to such an unexpected salvo?

"Er - what exactly do you mean by that Mr. Jones?" I returned, wondering what I had done to merit the comment.

"Well," he said. "During this session you've taken out a tooth, done two fillings, scaled and cleaned my teeth, and taken an impression for a denture."

"What's wrong with that?" I queried.

"You're not in a union are you?" he went on. "That's why I think you're a BF. You could have made four separate appointments to spread the work over a period. That would have increased your income and been better for me. As a union man I could have got four mornings off work and been paid for them by showing your appointment card."

I forget how I responded, if at all, to the piece of working-man's wisdom. It certainly gave me food for thought and an insight into the union-orientated society I was serving.

The National Health Service was fundamentally flawed by being run by overt politics. Your health is very personal to you and those who administer to your health needs should be dedicated to medicine in all aspects of humane caring, sympathy and understanding. Politicians in the round or in bulk are orientated to their political party and its beliefs or policies.

My entire training, every penny, had come from the sweat of my father and in no way had the State assisted me to start my Practice from scratch. It was successful due to my own efforts in my calling. The N.H.S. came in thro' the front door of my surgery and thereafter told me what to do and what fee I had to charge. I became a Civil Servant.

Chapter 12

THE BREAKDOWN - RESIGNATION

The extraordinary demand for dental treatment under the NHS continued into the early nineteen sixties before abating, while my own keen interest in the profession of dentistry had declined: I had become less willing to give my all in pursuit of excellence. The maxim 'do only what you have to do' was replacing the earlier ideal of 'only the best is good enough.' I still prided myself on work well done and maintained a high standard, but the excitement and challenge had gone.

One day in 1962 I received a telephone call from the Chairman of the Surrey Local Dental Committee. He told me that he had just become privy to a backstairs intrigue to vote me off the committee at that evening's meeting.

Needless to say, this little bombshell set me back on my heels. I had been on that committee since 1948, when I had led it in opposition to joining the NHS. Since then there had been many spirited sessions and the inevitable clashes of opinion, most of them good-natured. What was going on now behind the scenes sounded like an organised campaign against me. Why? Perhaps I had spoken my mind once too often and antagonised somebody who was now thirsting for revenge. The reason hardly mattered. To have attended the meeting would have aggravated matters unnecessarily. This game had rules like any other, and nobody knew better than I what they were. I sat down in the surgery to write a note of resignation to the Chairman, and on my way home, called in at his house to hand it to him.

Thinking about it later, I felt a sense of deprivation. I could now understand better how my father must have felt when in my youth he was ousted from the Secretaryship of the local Wesleyan Chapel Council after 26 years of dedicated service. I could see him before me, devastated by my mother's death two years before I qualified, when my sister Enid and I took him to Bournemouth for a week to help him face the future. In due course he had re-married, and barely three years later, in 1952, I had received a garbled telephone message from my step-mother that he had suffered an embolism and died ten minutes after.

At his funeral I was overcome with grief for the passing of one who had been my example of all that a man should be. He was my dearest friend, from whom I drew strength, and for the first time in my life and at the age of forty I had felt alone and fearful of the future. Neither he nor my mother had the comfort of their only son's presence in their last hours and it was always a matter of deep regret to me that I should have been hundreds of miles away by the disposition of fate.

Now, ten years after his death another link with my past had been severed. I knew I would miss the company of my colleagues, few of whom I ever met outside of the committee meetings. But for the support of my wife, a gentle and loyal person, I would have found it difficult to cope with the isolation I felt.

The insidious growth of inflation, a relatively new term to seize the news headlines, was undermining many a dental practice. The resultant, steady increase in costs was belatedly recognised by the Labour Government in awards of 2% in dentist's fees - a derisory amount when inflation was running at many times that figure. But what else should we have expected when Denis Healey, a prospective Labour Prime Minister and one of the party's most powerful men, shouted from the rostrum at a Party Conference, 'We shall squeeze the rich until the pips squeak'? Someone had obviously told the policy-makers that dentists were to be numbered among the wicked men exploiting the workers for gain. The plain fact was that the average, conscientious dentist earned less after paying his surgery and other expenses than those sacred cows of the unions - the dockers and newspaper printing workers. My own annual turnover hovered around £6,000 gross for years, while inflation roared away. Yes, I had a nice house on mortgage, but only a frugal way of life enabled me to save for retirement.

I could not have known that matters were soon to be taken out of my hands. It began with an appointment at an Ear, Nose & Throat clinic, made at my own request, to straighten the bridge of my nose - the result of a minor accident while in the RAF. This somehow gave rise to catarrhal sinus infection, fluid on my chest, and pulsating headaches - a condition diagnosed as bronchiecstasis.

Given my generally unfortunate experiences with the medical profession, it was perhaps inevitable that the GP should pronounce that the infection stemmed from my chest, whereas I was sure it originated in my nose. He was convinced that a course of antibiotics would cure it, while I urged that the side-effects of such treatment, then not fully researched, could invalidate any cure.

Unhappily he won the day, and for the next year, five different antibiotics were tried, each one failing in turn to give more than temporary relief. When I was transferred to the Kingston-upon-Thames Chest Clinic, the specialist there colluded with my GP to prescribe further antibiotics.

It all built up to a crisis one Saturday morning in 1968 when I was in my garden with two Scottish medical friends, and suddenly keeled over, gasping for breath. The frightening experience passed, and when feeling recovered later in the day I set off for Farnham with these two friends and my wife. There, inexplicably, I collapsed again and had to be helped to a seat in a draper's shop on the corner of Downing Street.

By now I was really worried. My medical friends were in no doubt as to the cause - side-effects from the various antibiotics, resulting in massive concentrations of fluid in my chest that were resistant to being coughed up.

The condition became worse, with no cure in sight. I had to commute daily to the surgery, and daily it became harder to do so. Constant bouts of nervous dyspepsia and difficulty in breathing made surgery work all but impossible. My GP, as usual, had the answer. "Your dilation is very low and you could fall flat on your back at any time. You should sell the practice and retire on grounds of disability."

Such was my physical and emotional state that there seemed to be no alternative. The sale of my beloved practice was put in train and the three months notice required by the NHS was given. At least it seemed as though I would be compensated, since two Surrey colleagues had expressed interest in buying the practice I was so proud of and which I had nurtured over the years.

With six weeks of the NHS three months notice gone, the Labour

Government suddenly announced the infamous 'freeze on capital', which sent the country's financial institutions into turmoil. Overnight, Bank Rate rose from 9% to 14%, and the business community prepared itself for a new Ice Age. With the contract for the sale of my practice drawn up and ready for signature, both prospective buyers withdrew, unable to face the more than 50% increase in interest rates on the loan they were about to take.

This development shattered my confidence completely. The fact that I was obliged by contract to complete all outstanding treatment in six weeks was an overwhelming prospect in my weakened conditon.

Meanwhile the terms of my severance from the NHS had been agreed. That is to say, I was told what I would receive; a tax-free sum of £640 and a pension of £780 p.a. No doubt the authorities based their parsimonious figures on the supposition that the sale of the practice would compensate me adequately. If so, they could not have been more wrong. I found myself unable to carry out the outstanding work in the surgery to satisfy NHS requirements, and with the freeze on capital and exorbitant interest rates, I eventually had to sell the practice at a ridiculously low figure to a most unsuitable man, the only prospective buyer, and raise my own mortgage for him to buy it! It almost broke my heart to leave that happy practice and a surgery that at times rang with laughter; a bitter end to twenty four years of sustained work.

My medical condition only began to improve after a heated argument with the Chest Consultant at Kingston Hospital. I told him that if I could just give myself a 'proof puncture' to relieve the congestion caused by the infected sinuses that I was sure was the root cause of my trouble, I could 'sort myself out.'

He saw this as a slight to his professional competence, and angrily telephoned the ENT department, requesting that I be examined forthwith. I was seen without delay, and poured out my tale of woe to the surgeon who, examining me, agreed with my own diagnosis. "I'll arrange for a proof puncture as soon as possible," he assured me.

"Look", I told him, "I've been messed about by these fatuous people for over a year. Please will you do it now, or let me? I've carried out this treatment myself while in the RAF."

He saw the sense of the argument and promptly carried out the local operation that involves anaesthetising the membrane in the nose (the antrum) that protects the sinus cavity, puncturing it with a hollow needle, and washing out the cavities with a saline solution.

Following this treatment, the improvement in my chest condition was almost immediate. I did not see the Chest Consultant again, and if I had done so, I should have left him in no doubt as to my opinion of his sheer incompetence.

That year of 1968 was a watershed in my life. My illness and the loss of the practice were in themselves hard enough to come to terms with, but the year also saw the deaths of my wife's much loved brother, my dental mechanic and, hardest of all, my close friend from Edinburgh days, John McConville. It was John, practising in Croydon, who with Phil Mellish in nearby Surbiton, between them helped with urgent cases during my 1957 illness and organised a locum. I shall never forget John's sad comment on his deathbed with an incurable brain tumour. "You know, Wick, it was our misfortune to be born thirty years too late."

To be forced into retirement at the age of 56 through sheer inability to cope with the day-to-day work I had been trained to do was a shock. I was not ready for the changes in routine, and I missed the stimulus of my patients, whose problems outside dentistry they would often confide in me. I was no longer important. Nobody apart from my wife depended on me.

As the weeks went by I became morose and bad-tempered - a veritable trial to my long-suffering spouse, whom sometimes in my mind I would resolve to divorce as an alternative to leaving her a widow by my own hand. I wandered through the garden, talking to the trees, reliving my life and wondering how I could have avoided the misery I had brought upon myself.

It was a chance remark that began to change things. I had annoyed my wife more than usual and she retaliated "If you hadn't spent all those hundreds of pounds on your plants, we would not be so hard up as we are now."

I was furious at the time, but what she said was true enough. I estimated that I had spent at least £2,000 on various plants at Runfold - money that would have helped bridge the gap between my pension and the cost of maintaining our expensive property with its high rates and a mortgage that still had two years to run when I left the NHS. Supposing I were to cultivate - take cuttings and grow on - certain species to market commercially. The more I thought about that, the better it looked.

I needed something constructive to occupy me, a plan of action to give me the routine of ordered activity I so missed. If I could just earn enough to cover the original cost of those plants, I could show my wife that the hobby she criticised was at least self-supporting. So, with something to aim for at last, I began making enquiries to establish the best way of going about my new business venture.

. . . . . .

We had fallen in love with the house when we first saw it in 1949 after looking at dozens of others. It was set back from the Crookesbury Road that runs from Runfold to Elstead, and the name "Freeland" suited it well. A long, thin parallelogram extending to four acres, the woodland site supported Silver Birch, Mountain Ash, Scots Pine and later Rhododendrons and Azaleas in profusion on its acid soil. The far boundary abutted a bridle path, used by the horsey fraternity, where I would stride among the bracken and indigenous pines on my way across Moor Park to the River Wey.

Often one of our Sealyham dogs would nose its way into a badger sett, whereupon the enraged Mr. Brock would charge out in pursuit, stopping only when he saw me and my stick. Alas, within seven years all this land was built on, but I have many happy memories of that wilderness of pine and bracken. Beyond the bridle path was Bides Wood, in the middle of which stood a very tall pine - home for several successive years to a pair of Hen-Harriers. I would watch in wonderment the antics of the hen bird as she left the nest to intercept her mate on his return with food for the young. At the last moment before they met in mid-air she would flash beneath him, turn over on to her back, seize his offering in her talons, and wheel away back to the nest. As a display of precision aerobatics, it was endlessly fascinating.

Here in our garden was birdlife of astonishing variety. Virtually every species of woodland bird known in England visited us and nested in or around the place. Woodpeckers (all three), Nuthatches, Tree Creepers, Missel Thrushes, all the Titmouse family, Owls, Wrens, and even that smallest of all British birds, the Gold-Crested Wren, so light that you were hardly aware of its weight in your hand. They built their beautiful round nests in our conifers, to the delight of the greedy grey squirrels, who would wait until they could hear the nestlings calling before swarming up the tree, pulling down the nest, and gorging themselves on the young. I built many a wire-netting platform half-way up the tree, but invariably the squirrels bypassed it and got their meal.

The covey of partridges that appeared on the lawn shortly after our arrival soon fell prey to nearby shotguns, but the roe deer often to be seen cropping the grass in the early morning were welcome and frequent visitors. They never stayed long enough to be a nuisance among the plants, probably because my wife used to take the dogs on a daily walk, and their scent must have been everywhere.

Once we had agreed on an overall plan for the garden, we could make a start. Paths were the priority. We had actually bought four acres of woodland with a house and lawn - no garden as such. So the first tasks were to make paths to the designated planting areas. The widest of these, sufficient to take a car, ran along the boundary to the far fence. Other paths ran in and out of the trees. Straight paths, as every gardener knows, look too regimented, whereas a curve will trick the eye into an illusion of depth and suggest hidden pleasures beyond the next bend.

What we did not know until we started planting was that certain local residents would make it difficult to raise anything green. "Freeland" was home to a multitude of rabbits, not to mention untold hordes of wood-ants fully half an inch long and a generous sprinkling of moles. There were also hazards of a different kind which I shall come to later.

The terrain was a rabbit's Utopia; tall bell heather mixed with wild Wortleberry or Blaeberry in extensive patches, giving excellent ground cover; massive areas of bracken up to ten feet high as thick as a bamboo bed, and all on greensand that lent itself to burrowing. In this ideal environment, the rabbits had bred in numbers far beyond what any natural predators or my sixteen-bore shotgun could deal with. Noting that in my neighbours' gardens the flower beds were covered with one-inch mesh wire-netting, I prepared to follow their example in due course, once the plants were established.

I had spent several weekends clearing a patch from the top wood of about 90 yards (or metres) long by 8 wide, to create a vista I could enjoy from my bedroom window. I visualised a mini-Capability Brown avenue of trees with a grass walk between. With this in mind I had purchased some two dozen special trees, twelve for each side, digging out well-prepared planting holes. The following day, Sunday, I got the trees all planted, finishing well into the early December twilight.

I rushed into the garden next morning after breakfast to view my precious plants before setting off for the surgery, but when I arrived at the clearing I could hardly believe my eyes. Every one of those lovely little trees had been chewed - all the top leading shoots nipped off, side branches missing, some eaten to a mere six inches above ground.

To say I was angry and disappointed would be a gross understatement. I brooded over this orgy of destruction all day long, and if any of my patients had been awkward, they would have felt the sharp edge of my tongue very quickly!

Sometimes a hard lesson is necessary to put a brake on one's ambitions. Thereafter, no tree was planted without a high wire netting cage around it. We put this principle to work when we planted a vegetable patch near to the back door and surrounded it with three-foot high, one-inch mesh wire-netting. One morning, we looked out to see the patch as bare as Mother Hubbard's cupboard. Obviously the enemy was not going to be beaten so easily. Further serious thought eventually produced a brainwave. I would build a garden wall all round my proposed vegetable plot. That would solve the problem, provide shelter form the worst of the wind, and look decorative too.

My only mistake was to assume that all I had to do was to assemble the materials, find a bricklayer, and make a start. I had reckoned without the bureaucracy of the Labour Government, requiring all sorts of permits for materials and labour claimed to be in short supply five years after the end of the war, while busily giving away parts of our Empire and opening the floodgates of immigration, therby compounding the problems of supply. Without going into details, I can say that after many frustrating delays (it was round about the time that I was invited to bribe a civil servant to obtain a Hardy Spicer transmission coupling for my car, you may remember) I bought the nine thousand bricks I needed and located a 'brickie', who undertook to come along on Sunday mornings until the job was finished.

A year of Sunday mornings later, the wall had been built on suitable foundations with me acting as mate, mixing the cement and sometimes laying bricks too. It was a fine structure - a square sixty feet by sixty of single-skin brickwork buttressed by pillars five feet high and incorporating two arched gateways. Unfortunately the first heavy rain saturated the porous bricks, manufactured for internal partitions in houses, facing bricks with their hard skins being virtually unobtainable. My brickie then came up with a practical way to protect the wall. Two thousand very hard Midhurst Whites were obtained, a thousand of which capped the wall with a further two courses all round, and the remaining thousand went to build an extension wall to enclose an adjacent piece of land, designated for cultivation, the enclosure having a wrought iron gate between two five-foot pillars of brick. It all looked very nice, which is more than could be said for my bank balance afterwards!

At the end of this new piece, which we called the Coronation Garden (it was finished in 1952), I planted a Yew hedge from self-sown seedlings found on the Pilgrim's way nearby. In the same vicinity could be found the largest specimen of a very rare tree, a Variegated Plane, *Platanus Suttneri,* a sight to behold with its creamy white leaves fluttering in the wind and entirely filling the front garden of a semi-detached country cottage facing Puttenham Common. My haul of seedling yews, carefully dug up, was two dozen of about one foot high, and two splended three-footers. These two I manured particularly well so they would arch over a solid oak gate I planned to install between them.

Making a garden must be one of the most satisfying activities anybody can embark upon. God-like, one can make the desert flower if the ways of Nature are understood and accommodated. In much the same way as an artist must study his subjects before portraying them, so I made it my enjoyable business whenever possible to view as many famous gardens as I could discover. My wife and I spent very many happy hours at such magnificent locations as Bodnant, Baulkley Mill, Hidcote, Westonbirt, Kew, Blenheim Palace, etc. Think of a well-known garden, and we would have visited it, making notes of height, spread and site conditions of particular specimens for future reference.

We also derived much enjoyment from reading, particularly the classic "Making Love to Mother Earth" by A.A. Thomas. "A Garden in Wales" (A.T. Johnson), "The Well Tempered Garden" (C. Lloyd), and later "Better Gardening" by Robin Ian Fox, were others I can wholeheartedly recommend. When decision time came, I usually consulted a local nurseryman. My own favourites were then and are still the books on trees by Alan Mitchell, surely the most eminent authority on the subject in the country, and a man I was often in touch with in later years, a frequent visitor to my garden.

At the time of enclosing the area to be known as the "Coronation Garden", I had already planted there one of the first examples of the American Dawn Redwood, or *Metasequoia Glyptostroboides,* which Hilliers had grown from seed imported from the USA. A deciduous conifer, it was also unusual in having a distinctive, deeply recessed bole that when polished with an old leather gardening glove took on the appearance and patina of mahogany. When Alan Mitchell carried out a survey on the genus some years later, he told me my tree had the most deeply recessed bole of the fifty or so he had examined. It had another characteristic in that if the low branches are trimmed back to within about three inches of the trunk, instead of cutting the branch off flush to prevent rot creeping back, new shoots will sprout from here, making it easy to strike a new tree from cuttings. One such, taken by my brother-in-law, is now a stately sixty-footer in a Bradford park.

Another rarity worth mention was the true Cypress, *Cypress Cashmeriana*, which at a height of twenty-five feet became the tallest specimen in South-East England. It is supposed to be very tender, but it twice took twenty-six degrees of frost in its stride, though it went very brown in the process. Normally one would have considered it as dead as it looked, but any reader lucky enough to have one of these lovely trees should not despair or chop it down. It could come again as late as early July. Even rarer was my *Abies Kawakamii*, which I had planted too near the *Metasequoia* and it had to move - fortunately without losing it.

Our walled garden allowed us to cultivate marvellous crops of vegetables without feeding the ever-hungry rabbits, who were soon to be decimated by the scourge of myxomatosis. But we still had much to learn about the other pests. When we had made the clearing in the indigenous birch and bracken, I proudly planted on either side of the path two dozen special Camellias. These I had obtained from Gillian Carlyon at Tregrehan, St. Austell, about 1954, who had kindly taken Audrey and me round her extensive Rhododendron and Camellia garden. She was just starting to propagate using the innovative "mist" system, which we discussed at length. She was very proud of the American hybrids she had brought back from a trip to the USA. Her favourite seemed to be *Marjorie Magnificum,* and she was kind enough to pick out a couple of dozen of what she considered her best plants for us to take back to Surrey.

I duly planted these with great care beneath the obligatory wire cages, watered generously each summer at least twice a week and awaited the results. All that happened after three years was that one of them died. Of course I blamed myself for not giving it enough water, and left it there, hoping it would come again from the base.

One Sunday, realising that the others had scarcely grown in the four years they had been there I decided to dig up the dead one. What a shock! There was no shortage of root growth. I exhumed two large buckets full - but none of it Camellia root! It had all come from the Birches, as I found by digging, and the same was true for all the other Camellias. The phenomenon I had uncovered was a characteristic of the Birch on sandy soil, the culprits being mostly the *pubescens* variety and not the real Silver Birch, *Betula Alba Verrucosa.*

We set about clearing every remaining Birch from the vicinity and must have taken down nearly a hundred. It seemed that they had almost infinite capacity to send out roots just below the surface of the ground in search of moisture, thereby choking virtually everything in their path. In diligently following up and digging out all their roots, I traced one right back to the parent tree. Believe it or not, it measured no less than twenty-one yards. And there was I, diligently watering my Camellias for the benefit of those hungry trees! I replanted all the Camellias, whereafter they thrived, and cut up the Birches for burning on the wood fires in the house that satisfied all our heating requirements.

The wood-ants I mentioned earlier featured in another discovery. I had been given a very rare seedling tree, *Abies Faberei*, almost unobtainable today. Fully aware of its value, I planted it in a safe place but en route to the potting-shed and the house, giving me an opportunity to keep it under observation. Eventually it came to be taken for granted, until on one journey across the garden I stopped to look at it properly, and when I did so, the penny dropped. It looked just the same as it had always done! After several years, my little beauty was undeniably stunted in growth, doing nothing more than holding its own. But why?

Digging out the small conifer with great care - it was my rarest tree - I soon became aware of the ants, coming up from around the stem at ground level. The more I dug and shook the tree, the greater became the number of ants issuing forth. I noticed that the stem from ground level carried a series of cuts, that spiralled upwards, some of them deep enough to have penetrated through the bark, severing the cambium layer and thereby restricting the supply of sap. I suspected that the ants, in planting among its leaves the aphids that they cleverly "farm" and massage daily for their milk, had been running up and down the tree from their cosy nest in the roots, causing the damage to the bark by the incessant tramping of their tiny feet.

I was so incensed with the damage they had done to my precious tree that I dug it up and denuded the roots of every particle of soil before replanting it in another position, where sadly it soon died. What I should have done, I realised much later, was to have put down a poison for the ants and at the same time filled up the striations on the bark with grafting wax to promote callus for protection and regeneration of new bark, allowing the sap to flow unhindered again.

In a tree, the cambium layer of tissue lies between bark and heartwood and carries the sap, much as a blood-vessel carries oxygenated blood to all parts of our bodies. If this layer is damaged by a cut in the protective bark during Spring and Summer, the tree will exude sap, as a limb will ooze blood. And like the human tooth, a damaged tree will bring to the site certain specialised cells via the sap coming down from the leaves with its component chlorophyll. This greenish substance has a function similar to haemoglobin in the blood and is the essential catalyst in the formation of scar tissue or callus, which generally starts to form above the gash in the bark and spreads from there. It contains microscopic canals, just as dentine, and cementum in a tooth and its roots enable blood, lymph and nerve to circulate for the nourishment of the whole tooth. The healing process is one of many similarities between teeth and trees.

It would be fair to say that the biggest single problem at "Freeland" after coping with nature's plagues was keeping my plants damp, and it was aggravated by what Audrey saw as my obsessive plantings. The Surrey greensand, which with patient husbandry enabled me to grow specimen trees, azaleas and rhododendrons, would not retain moisture. Nevertheless in 1953 one project I accomplished was to clear the ground ready for a new wood that comprised 600 trees, with some fine specimens of Dunkeld Larch in the middle of it. As I brought new areas of woodland into cultivation, so I increased the need for watering.

Part of my grand scheme for the garden included the construction of pools, formed in concrete to a saucer-shaped design to resist the enormous pressures of expanding ice in winter that afflicted conventional rectangular structures. These worked extremely well for the wildlife and were much appreciated in hot weather by the grass snakes and smooth snakes which I forbade any of my part-time occasional gardeners to kill on pain of instant dismissal. But the pools could not supply water to the whole garden, and I had to fall back on the time-honoured hose, of which I had more than a quarter of a mile but which could only be secured to the one outside tap. My summers seemed to be spent in watering and grass-cutting, and between those tasks there was virtually no time to sit on the lawn in the sun and admire my creation. As things turned out, the experience of taming the wilderness I had so innocently taken on, and the hours spent in the potting shed and greenhouse, were to be the means of my salvation when everything I had worked for in my profession collapsed through my own debility.

. . . . . .

Necessity is the mother of invention, and so it was in my case. The few household items of value that we owned had been sold at Christie's for a few hundred pounds to supplement the inadequate pension, and our savings diminished month by month. With no prospect of employment, my enquiries among nurserymen at first suggested that the idea of making money by selling plants that had to be sold again at a profit was not feasible. The figure of £2,000 seemed like wishful thinking. First, the plants had to be of a popular type and variety. It was no good growing only what I liked myself. Buyers also needed to know that they were healthy, free from any blight or disease and with good potential. Then they had to be available in quantity, and the price low enough to be tempting.

With all this, I did eventually find my first buyer, then a second and a third. I worked hard and systematically, building up my contacts until I was supplying seven buyers scattered over Surrey, Hampshire, Sussex and London.

What surprised me most was the callousness of the men who bought my plants when it came to taking them out of the soil. Mostly they were hacked about, chopped out carelessly, left lying about, and then flung into the lorry. Some of these plants must have been dead or dying before they left my property. No doubt the retail mark-up was high enough to withstand a few casualties.

Only one person displayed professional care; a woman arboriculturalist from an arboretum at West Dean near Chichester, who personally supervised her helpers and very carefully dug out and loaded some of the plants herself. This experience and others persuaded me that women are generally far more sensitive in their handling of living things than men.

It took almost two years of unremitting work to reach and then exceed my original figure. By that time I was aware of a big change in myself; not in physical fitness but in my attitude towards life and self-perception. The shadow of insanity, which at the time of retiring from my practice was real enough to have caused some colleagues to urge a course of electro-therapy at Brookwood Mental Institution, had passed. I could now face myself again, accept my limitations as an individual but with renewed confidence. I missed the challenge of dentistry and the daily routine. I had proved to my wife that I could grow and sell plants commercially and restored much faith in my own future.

In 1970 I felt well enough to renew our long-standing links with Cornwall, and confident enough to invest £4,500 of my savings to buy a lovely old cottage at Ruan Major on the Lizard. Appropriately named "Sunny Corner", its boundaries were thick with sixty-foot elms. These formed the subject of my enquiry to the Forestry Commission in Alic Holt, Farnham, as to whether these trees, situated in remote Cornwall, could be subject to the fearful Dutch Elm Disease. "Oh no," I was assured, "Cornish Elms are immune from it."

So they were, until they all got it! Before that unhappy event, I was already preparing to return to Dentistry if only I could think of a way to circumvent the National Health Service.

Chapter 13

ROYAL MILITARY POLICE

Another year passed before I actually did something about rejoining my former profession. I've always found the saying 'nothing ventured, nothing gained' relevant to my own experience, so I placed an advertisement in the British Dental Journal. It read 'Dentist requires post within 30 miles of Farnham, Surrey, not in NHS. Retired from own practice due to ill-health'.

The response to this was most encouraging. One of the replies was from the Royal Military Police at Roussillon Barracks, Chichester, just within the limit I had set myself as the furthest I wished to travel. An interview was arranged, and within three weeks of the advertisement's appearing, I began work with the Army Dental Corps, commuting on a much less hazardous run than the journey to the heavily-populated suburbs of London that had been my lot for twenty years.

The salary was very attractive for the three days weekly I was required to attend the Barracks. More important than that for my peace of mind was the feeling of being 'back in harness', doing a job I still loved in spite of the cost to my health levied by the bureaucratic workings of the NHS. I set out on the first morning with high hopes and on being met at Sick Quarters by a Mrs. Avery, could not help noticing the waiting-room was flagged with real stone and highly polished. Obviously they believed in 'spit and polish' in this barracks. As I strode confidently across the floor, my leather-soled brogues skidded on the slippery surface, my feet went up in the air, and I landed on my back with a resounding thump.

Mrs. Avery, dear lady, (we still exchange Christmas greetings) calmed me with a cup of tea. I was very shaken, but luckily not hurt, apart from some bruising. Shortly after, my 'Nurse' walked in, looking unlike any nurse or receptionist I'd ever seen. She got herself rigged out in a flowery black chiffon affair with a fringe on the sleeeves and at the bottom of the dress, and bedecked with beads. She would have cut a figure at a Buckingham Palace garden party. My mouth fell open and stayed open for longer than politeness allowed, I fear. No sooner had I begun to come to terms with the apparition than in marched the Adjutant, announced by a corporal with much stamping of feet and saluting. "The Commanding Officer presents his compliments and would be pleased to meet you, Mr. Dentist," the Adjutant proclaimed. "If it is convenient, perhaps you would kindly come with me now to Headquarters."

There I was duly introduced to Col. Salt. He struck me as a genuine person, a true gentleman, and in the years I spent under his charge, I never had cause to change that opinion. Another officer I met later who impressed me was attached to the Provost Marshal's unit in London. I did not see much of him, but had the opportunity of taking a professional look inside his mouth. To my surprise I saw some of the finest dental conservation work I had ever come across, made even more intriguing by his assurance that it had been carried out by a Chinese dentist in Hong Kong.

At first it was a novelty to feel free from the pressures I was accustomed to. Instead of cramming in 27 appointments on most working days, I was seeing a maximum of seven patients, leaving large slices of time unallocated that I did not know how to fill. Frequently, the person booked for an appointment failed to turn up, so that I had even more time on my hands. It was a situation I had never encountered in my working life previously, and I began to wonder how long I could accept the generous salary and tax-free travelling allowances which in my estimation I was certainly not giving value for.

On several occasions, sheer frustration caused me to write a letter of resignation, pointing out that there was not enough work for me and that I had been used to putting in a full day at my surgery. Each time I tore up the letter and resolved to soldier on. After all, the problems were inherent in the system. In the Air Force I had the authority to put any aircraftsman on a charge who failed to report for dental treatment. As a civilian I lacked such authority and an ex-RAF Squadron-Leader cut practically no ice in a peace-time military establishment. Moreover, at 59 I was at least a generation older than the average Army Dental Officer. All in all, I decided to stay and to count my blessings, not least of which was cooperation of my nurse-receptionists, who after the first unsuitable candidate, proved to be encouragingly helpful.

Among those deserving special mention were Mary Foister and June Brumpton, both of whom have visited me in my retirement on several occasions. They made my stint with the RMP very worthwhile though I must admit that the great advantage of that position was that it provided an adequate income with spare time. I was actually able to spend longer each week in my garden than at dental surgery! My salary increased progressively, as did my index-linked Health Service pension, which quadrupled in seven years with inflation and without further effort on my part. The irony of it all struck me forcibly. I was then earning more than at any time during my twenty years of hard labour in the NHS, without all the surgery expenses, the pressures and the drain on my health. If only it could have happened earlier!

The garden at "Freeland" flourished with the extra care I was able to lavish upon it. Everywhere the rabbits were being cut down by myxomatosis, and almost overnight new green growth was springing up free from their depredations. I found it easier to bring new areas of woodland under cultivation, and continued to experiment with different strains of rhododendrons and azaleas. Seasons came and went, each with its own special character in the garden, and in some ways it was the best time of my life.

During my seventh year at Chichester, news came that Her Majesty the Queen would visit the town to take over as C. in C. of the Royal Military Police Regiment as Roussillon Barracks. The date set for this occasion was March 10th 1977, and as usual with such events, it was broadcast through all the media. Inevitably the IRA was listening, and five weeks before the planned visit a bomb exploded in the Sergeants' Mess for the 1st Battalion of Parachute Regiment at Aldershot.

There was consternation at the RMP Barracks. For various reasons the visit could not be postponed, yet the main entrance was open to the road from Chichester to Midhurst and the public would be gathering there in hundreds. It would be an ideal opportunity for an IRA sympathiser to take a pot shot at the Queen, especially as one of her undertakings was in connection with the statue of a mounted military policeman which was within 15 yards of this main road, right in front of the guard room.

In the Mess I overheard that an approach had been made to a famous nursery at Winchester for an estimate to landscape a free-standing plant bed between the main gate and this statue. The figure given was many hundreds of pounds, but the funds available did not rise to such heights. The idea was that if this large bed, eight yards by seven yards, could be filled with big evergreens it would shield the Queen from a possible trouble-maker. It seemed to me that I had the capabilities of undertaking this scheme, using the plants in my garden, so I went to see the C.O. and the officer delegated to be in charge of flower beds, grass and outside effects. My offer was accepted and the officer visited my garden to see what I proposed to do. It was agreed that the Army would supply the necessary transport and men to load.

Although this big bed at the main gate was the lynch-pin, it transpired that six other beds between the Guard Room and the Officers Mess needed to be transformed from a mass of half dead rose trees and shrubs lost in weeds. These I also undertook to sort out into something suitable for a Queen to look at on her way to and from the Mess. I figured out that this undertaking would take me ten full days of work - six days to dig out the plants and four to get the beds planted up. My estimate had assumed that I should get some help at the Barracks. The main problem was the date, March 10th. In Sussex no flowering shrub would be in flower and the weather could be as cold as charity. Seven beds for the Queen to look at, without a flower in sight, was a pretty tall order for any amateur gardener, the more so when the plants for this big free-standing bed at the main gate needed to be evergreens at least 14 feet high and thick in foliage

I gave a lot of thought to the problem and ended up with lists of times, places and plants, just about papering the walls. My wife really thought I was in for another mental aberration and said so, but eventually I could see what was needed. There would be five large conifers from 12 to 15 feet and another seven from 9 to 12 feet to create the two back rows. Getting these big fellows out of the ground, wrapped up in hessian, tied and balled and then shifted many hundreds of yards to the gathering place for loading on to the army lorries was in itself a job for half a dozen blokes; doing it by myself on the selected day was almost too much.

I had fortunately devised a method of getting large plants out of the ground and also a 'skid' to shift them once out. The lifting apparatus, more a 'contraption', mainly consisted of a metal framework using an old garden hammock and a mini hoist. The 'skid', after many improvements, arrived at a Mark 7 version, basically using a 4 x 2 sheet of ½" corrugated plastic sheet, with pulling facilities and hose-pipe runners, which had helped me move many hundreds of plants and saved me from rupturing myself or worse.

After six days of working every daylight hour, I had dug up, wrapped up, pulled, tugged and shifted ready for loading something near 270 plants, not all to go in the three army lorries but some to be taken each day in my Morris 1000 Traveller. The party of eight soldiers with these army vehicles proved utterly useless at loading and I had to undertake this chore myself in order to pack 'em in and to save them from serious damge. Two army lorries came on the Sunday afternoon, the working party having had lunch en route and washing it down with something stronger than mineral water, so that putting my precious plants into the lorry was an off-duty, half-cut, hilarious lark, which will explain why with a complement of seven able-bodied young soldiers I was the only one doing anything in a responsible manner! Going down on the Monday morning in my car loaded up to the roof with plants which I had not risked in the lorry, I passed the army lorry on its way to pick up another load at my garden, but before they returned to the barracks it was well past midday. So my planned start at setting out these plants was thrown off schedule right from the outset and in fact the physical hardship I was forced to undergo was entirely due to the useless hands put at my disposal on the first day and a half.

The second day I was helped by the official gardener at the barracks and we got on fine and made good progress. I also had a useful young soldier helper who had had some experience of using a spade by helping his father on his allotment. But on the following day, after I had dealt with the Sick Parade and was changing into my gardening togs, a knock at the surgery door announced a Staff Sergeant who had been sent by the RSM to inform me that this helpful young soldier would not be helping me any more. He had been transferred to more important work! However, six other men were to be placed at my disposal.

The next set-back was something I had not anticipated. On inspecting the five beds set between the Guardroom and the Officers Mess I was horrified to discover that they consisted mainly of masses of stones, including great chunks of rock. Now I realised why these beds had only tatty roses and shrubs in them. To dig a hole to plant anything was a pick-axe job, yet here was I with enough plants to fill these beds. Oh yes, I had men equipped with spades, but believe it or not, none of them could dig out a hole. They just handed the spade to me, saying 'I can't get the spade in because of the stones'. So I sent one of the soldiers to find the gardener and a pick-axe. Back he came to say there *was* a pick-axe, but the handle was broken!

There was no other course but to dig out these blocks of stone and cement using a garden fork, and the quickest way to do it was to have the fork in my own hands. I have always maintained that before you plant a bed or border it must first be cleared of weeds, roots and any heavy stones, etc, otherwise you are doing the equivalent of brushing the rubbish under the carpet or slapping paint on a wall covered with dirt or grease. You thereby waste time and money in doing a botched job.

My temper was not improved when I found that the one young soldier who had shown gardening ability and willingness had been taken from me in order to serve the Queen at lunch, and was now undergoing special training inside the Officers Mess whilst I who was old enough to have been his grandfather, was sweating like a galley-slave outside. I could easily have served the Queen myself without any special training but nobody among all these able-bodied young men could offer me, who needed it most, the practical help I had been promised. The one bright feature in the gloom was the weather. Fine, sunny and mild, it was almost too good to be true.

It was on the Thursday, my last day to finish the last three beds, including the most important, the large half-moon one outside the Officers Mess and which I had designated 'The Queen's Bed' as I was putting in all my special plants, that I nearly despaired. I arrived at the barracks loaded up to the gunwales in my Morris Traveller, already late and dead on my feet, to be met as I was turning in at the main gate by a troop of Mounted Horse. Out rushed the RSM directing me in language richly laced with expletives, to draw up on to the pavement and to stop there.

All at once I seemed to be surrounded with the Military, all armed, and all I could do was to sit there helplessly cursing myself for not being inside before this full dress rehearsal took place. Then out came the band, blowing its heart out, followed by ranks of men and a very big draft of the Women's Military Police, swinging their arms fit to split their tunics and being bawled at by their NCOs who seemed to be competing with the blasting of the band. Then somebody let off a firecracker, I presume to see if any of the horses would play up.

At last my vigil on the pavement came to an end with the RSM waving me in. I returned to my surgery for a sandwich lunch, leaving all my plants and gear on the path by the 'Queen's Bed', but when I returned the whole scene had changed. The beds were surrounded by military and the path lined with soldiers with fixed bayonets. About two hundred were bunched on the grass to represent the civilian onlookers, the band at the ready and the mounted troop nearby - to resounding orders of 'Attention' and royal salutes and the band belting out the National Anthem. Out of the Officers Mess stepped Mrs. Provost Marshal' playing the part of the Queen, flanked by the Provost Marshal himself and the General in charge of the Royal Military Police Regiment and the troops playing the part of the civilian onlookers being bawled at: 'Cheer, you silly buggers'. Everybody was in full ceremonial and number-one uniforms, while I in my gardening attire had a grandstand view of this bit of dress rehearsal.

Suddenly a stentorian voice behind me thundered 'Witherwick, you had better get all this finished by tonight, otherwise you could find yourself in the Tower!'

The Provost Marshal, Brigadier Matthews, was an imposing figure in his uniform, complete with sword. I did not need his half-humorous admonishment to convince me that I should spare no effort to finish, and finish I did, when I could not see to do any more, and then found it most difficult on the drive home not to fall asleep.

Next morning we made a very early start, as all ticket holders had to arrive by 8.30 a.m., allowing time for a thorough search for hidden weapons as we edged slowly past the checkpoint, where my wife's handbag was emptied out and her underwear looked into!

No doubt the ceremony would have been more enjoyable had I not been so tired. My reward was in seeing those beds proudly decked out with my own plants. The Royal Military Police made me the guest of honour at a special lunch in the Mess, when a very nice presentation was made to me by the Provost Marshal after he had first leant across the table and asked if I would not now accept some monetary payment for my efforts.

"No Sir," I replied, "I said it would be done for nothing as my contribution to the Queen's visit, and I'm not going to change my mind now."

How many amateur gardeners at the age of 65 could or would,

from their own garden and almost single handed, shift this lot 30 miles, re-plant and then dig up again to re-load back to their garden the very next morning after the Queen's visit? Surely no one else would be such a silly billy nowadays, when money so often seems to be the sole motivation for doing anything at all.

One other very different incident that stands out from those generally uneventful years was when I decided to extract a front tooth, an upper lateral, from a very difficult patient - myself! The tooth had lost its crown, leaving the root at gum level. It was a straightforward job. I had extracted hundreds like it. I had even taken out one of my own teeth previously, a three-rooter complete with abscess sac, with the assistance of my excellent nurse, Naidene Davies (now Mrs. White) who was the last nurse to join my NHS practice. The only difference now was that my close sight had deteriorated, obliging me to seek professional help from my friend Austin in Farnham. His prescription of half-lenses worked very well. Simply by looking over the top of them I could focus my distance vision, which was unimpaired.

So I made preparations in the surgery at the RMP Medical Centre to tackle this little job, ensuring that my nurse at the time, Mary Foister, was somewhere else, to enable me to work undisturbed. I set up a mirror on the bench next to the steriliser, gave myself an injection and waited. When I knew the area of operation was numb, I took up the forceps and began.

After a while I realised that I was not getting the forceps on to the root but into the jawbone, from which pieces were beginning to come away. I tried again, with the same result. It was mystifying. I was stone cold sober and behaving like one half-drunk. I began to get impatient, then to lose my temper, and still all I got out of my mouth were more pieces of jawbone.

I don't know how long I persisted with the lunacy. My mouth was literally a bloody mess. There was nobody I could call to for help, and the tooth had to come out before the anaesthetic wore off. Eventually the forceps must have gripped the root, one of the smallest in the mouth, and out came the tooth, but at what cost in time and temper, to say nothing of the damage to my jawbone!

The reader of this account might be tempted to think 'Why didn't the old fool stay in retirement? He must be as blind as a bat.' Well, my mistake was in placing the mirror too high. When I was looking at my mouth through it, I was peering over the top of my glasses, giving

160

me a very blured image. Had I been able to position the mirror lower, I would have had to look through the lenses, as I did when treating a patient. In the excitement of the moment, that elementay fact had quite escaped me.

I had begun to think somewhat wistfully of retirement, and over the following year or so Audrey and I looked at all the options. The garden at "Freeland" was laid out more or less to my satisfaction but during most of the year, represented a full-time commitment. In the summer the grass-cutting alone took me an average of six hours weekly, using the best machine available then (apart from the 'ride-on' variety that I wouldn't consider). This rotary mower, driven by a two-stroke engine, was 'The Windsor' model by Shay's of Basingstoke. It would cut anything from a hay field to a bowling-green, and could even be used to collect leaves. No longer made, my favourite machine is still in good working order.

It occurred to me that if we moved, much of the huge garden could be sold to a developer. Land in the area that was suitable for development fetched large sums. But if we stayed and kept a smaller garden, we would lose the privacy we valued so much.

1979 was the year when we finally decided to leave Surrey for Cornwall. This was an obvious choice for several reasons. We loved the county and already had a holiday property on the Lizard which, however, did not suit my ambitious gardening plans. A prime benefit was that living costs in Cornwall would be far lower than our outgoings in the London stockbroker commuter belt, which would eat into the pension that would be our main source of income.

Choosing and buying a suitable property was another matter. I heard about a remote river valley with 20 acres, which sounded like a dream, and at the right price. But like most good things, there were snags along the way. Indeed, the story of how I eventually came by it would almost fill another book. Suffice it to say that my success was due in no small part to the efforts of a Mr. Prior of Falmouth and Mylor, who 'kept his foot in the door' while I was still in Surrey.

It is amazing how many people come a cropper over buying property. They just don't seem to realise that business is business and sentiment is not part of it; that nothing is finalised until the Contract is signed and even then there's many a slip between cup and lip. As for selling houses, again ignorance is bliss. The value of the property is what it fetches in the open market, not what the owners think they ought to get. There's a right time and price for a sale, but they must complement each other. So often one sees property hanging about for a year or more - obviously over-priced. The penny drops eventually and the owners in desperation are prevailed upon to reduce their price considerably, but they still don't sell due to the fact that the few who would have bought at that time did not enquire as the price was too high, and now they have gone elsewhere.

But the real futility of these owners is when they do sell after two years at a much reduced price, the price they will have to pay for whatever they buy will be considerably higher than if they had sold their own two years previously at a realistic figure and bought another house then. I have sold four properties in my time, and in each case the property was sold within a short time of being put on the market; the time and the price was right, and that's business.

To fund the purchase of "Trelean" I sold three acres of the garden at "Freeland" with planning permission, and the house itself with the remaining acre of grounds - still a large garden by most standards. I also sold the Cornish Cottage and gave up my job with the Royal Military Police. At the end of all the wheeling and dealing, I had a substantial sum of money to my account. It was the best business deal I had ever negotiated, and a new phase in my life was about to begin.

Chapter 14

RETIREMENT - CORNWALL

There was no denying the logic of buying a house in Cornwall. On one item alone, the rates, we would save £700 yearly. Multiply that 1979 figure by eight and you will have roughly the equivalent in today's (1991) money. But you cannot move house after 30 years without a few problems, as we soon found out.

The enormous labour involved in digging up my favourite plants and preparing them for transplantation in Cornwall rivalled my efforts for the Queen's visit to Roussillon Barracks. By the day arranged for our removal, I had assembled four lorry-loads of trees and shrubs, with enough besides to fill my estate car seven times over. My plans for the uncultivated 20 acre valley demanded no less. Then there was all the furniture and household effects, including nearly forty packing-cases, awaiting the removal van.

After I had spent twenty minutes showing one man how to dismantle an antique wardrobe that was otherwise too big to come down the stairs, the foreman of this six-man team came to tell me that our belongings would not fit into the enormous vehicle they had brought, and that he would have to telephone for an additonal one. I was hardly surprised when he duly reported back to say that his firm had no other available. Later, however, a small van was procured to load the left-overs into overnight store at the firm's expense, to be sent to Cornwall the following day.

Audrey and I finally got away around 2.30 p.m., our Morris Estate loaded to the roof, and we drove non-stop to Honiton for the first half of our 260-mile journey. We took a welcome break there before

163

setting off again, arriving in Cornwall late at night.

We were at 'Trelean' the next morning at eight to be ready for the removal van that was travelling through the night. We waited with increasing frustration all the morning, not daring to leave for a meal in case the men arrived in our absence. All we could do in that empty house was to speculate on what had gone wrong.

At 2 p.m. we found out, when the removal van and men arrived with their tale of woe. While crossing Salisbury Plain the windscreen had shattered. They had waited four hours for a replacement before pushing on to Exeter, where the engine failed. Repairs having been made, they set off again, and now they were here, as famished as we were, apparently surprised that we were not able to knock up a meal for them there and then. Obligingly I raided the local shop and brought back enough to keep everybody sweet.

The morning had been sunny, ideal for the occasion, but the clouds were gathering overhead, and as we began unloading, down came the rain and later the snow. The end of that long day saw us tired, wet, and vowing never to move again.

It took us five or six weeks to settle into the big stone house and consider the consequences of our move. Here we were, a quarter of a mile from the nearest habitation, looking out over the middle reaches of the Helford river and the miniature river valley through which coursed the pure, fresh streams that supplied our domestic water. We had mains electricity but no gas or main sewer, and the house was heated by an oil-fired boiler, supplemented by an endless supply of wood. Dustbins had to be taken ninety yards to a point accessible to the Council dustcart and the approach to the property was via a very long, narrow, very steep high-banked lane that led nowhere else but was rampant with wild flowers in the spring and summer. With the nearest shop one mile away in the village, and Helston a further seven miles, the description 'remote' was appropriate. This demi-paradise, complete with ancient Cornish Long House and barn, was just what I had been looking for; a challenge to ward off any thoughts of old age and to enjoy the fruits of our labours when the work was done.

I will not bore the reader with a blow-by-blow account of how this wilderness was tamed. Suffice it to say that early on I decided that when my clearing and re-planting programme was complete, I would open it to the public so that others could share its wild beauty. The brief account that follows is one that I wrote three or four years ago and duplicated as a hand-out guide for visitors :-

TRELEAN: Something about the place

As far as is known at present, LEAN goes back to at least 1445, since it is marked on the big map of Cornwall hanging in the passage outside the Map Room of St. Michael's Mount Castle. Until 1915 it had always been part of the TRELOWARREN Estate, when it was then sold to the Richards, who had been Tenant Farmers at Lean for five generations, going back as far as 1775. Willie Richards*, now in his eighties, left Lean in 1968 having been born in the old Farmhouse which sits at the back of the farmyard, with its interconnection to the old Barn, with sounds of the cattle coming up to be heard in the end bedroom! The old Farmhouse remained thatched until the middle sixties.

The present Trelean House was built in 1901, and except for the granite plant troughs, all the stone used in its construction came from a Quarry on the cliff edge down by the Helford, behind the Croftwood, all the stone coming up the steep 1-in-5 incline by horse and cart.

It has been ascertained from a Tithe map dated 1845 that the lane from the Farmyard was known as DOODES LANE, and according to this map, the lane used to go straight on at the Viewpoint; the Roundel loop being made approx. 1875, in order to allow horse and cart easier access down to the beach to collect seaweed or bladder wrack and also sandy gravel. The Inlet at the beach is known on the river as Sandy Gap. It is worthy of note that where the old Doodes Lane came down over the back of the Roundel, it joined up with the Old Pack Horse Trail, which ran from St. Martin (here) and Mawgan. Two pieces of the Old Pack Horse Trail still remain in the area of the Croftwood; the Trail crossed Trelean Stream at a point where the lowest valley bridge is today.

The original Croft was thought to be sited at the East end of the Croftwood near to where a spring erupts in this area. It is most likely that the *Lean* originated from a family of this name, since it has been established that one of the parishioners called Leane was Baptised in Constantine Church in 1572 (see "Constantine in Cornwall", C. Henderson M.A. page 215). It is therefore no stretch of imagination to believe a Leane from this family came across the river and pitched his

* Unfortunately Willie Richards died in 1988, aged 87.

shack in the Croftwood, alongside the Pack Horse Trail and this spring, no doubt running his pigs in the oak wood hereabout and helping himself to the Squire's firewood and game for food and warmth, and paying a peppercorn rent when needs be. In any case, there was always fish in the river for those who knew how to catch them, with kindling wood to hand for the fry - still the best way to eat your fish, unless like the Japanese you prefer it raw, even all alive and kicking!

At the far end of the property going down river there is a Boundary Stone wall, now well covered with moss and over 400 yards long, overlooking Tremayne Quay and Creek. This wall was built by unemployed Tin Miners in the First World War, the stone taken from two pits seen at top and bottom, and their wages paid out of the pocket of Sir Courtney Vyvyan. It was another Vyvyan in 1886 who had Tremayne Quay built with its two mile drive to Trelowarren House, for Queen Victoria to step on to from the Royal Yacht Prince Albert, and thence to the house by horse and carriage. Some six years back the present Baronet Sir John Vyvyan gifted the Quay and Drive to the National Trust. Near where a good view is obtained of Tremayne Quay from the river walk, due to two oak trees which have recently fallen into the river, there is a well-concealed tunnel with access to the river, and which goes back across three fields to emerge below the Pool on Doodes Lane, no doubt used for nefarious activities away from the prying eyes of the Customs men. Much of this tunnel is now, however, impassable. Also by the riverside in this area stands a massive old oak, estimated to be on the 400 year mark, in a very good state of health; unfortunately its roots are being eroded of soil at high tides by the waves set up by big boats and speed boats going too fast, thus creating excessive disturbance on the shoreline. To my certain knowledge during the past six years five large trees have toppled off the edge into the river. It is therefore not inconceivable that what is probably one of the oldest oak trees in the County will finish its days in the river within the next fifty years. Conservation on a big beech tree, back along the river bank some fifty yards, has been undertaken whereby some seven tons of breast wood was removed, thus getting the balance of weight back on to the land side. However to do the same for this venerable oak would entail the removal of some 20 tons weight of breast wood, a self-appointed task of daunting consequence.

You climb up the hillside by the Boundary Wall, a stiff 1-in-5 climb, and pass under some very fine beech trees, mostly well over a hundred feet in height having exceptionally fine straight trunks; as you turn left at the top there is a beech on the boundary with the field, which could be over 300 years old. To obtain an approx. age of a forest tree, you measure at about 4½ feet its girth, and for those specimens enclosed, i.e. in a wood or forest, then ½ inch to a year is the norm; if the tree is exposed or isolated, then it is 1 inch to a year. Some good views as you emerge from the wood of the river and the Northern side of the Helford; Merthen Woods are directly opposite, mentioned in Domesday, and culminating in Groyne Point. This Point enables one to see the Head of the river to the sea, but it also divides the river from Polwheveral Creek. Your descent down the hillside is following what used to be a well-worn fox path, but now maintained for your easier passage.

None of the land lying behind the quarter mile of river frontage or the valley has ever been ploughed or brought into any form of cultivation for crops. In consequence the natural habitat has remained undisturbed, a natural sanctuary for mother nature, for trees, wild flowers, plants and ferns, insects and birds, so by keeping to the paths you enable this heritage to retain its privacy and age-old dignity. All that is being done is to add, wherever possible, further species of trees and plants to those already here.

Behind the pool on the right just before the path divides is a deep trench. Willie Richards used to watch his father and his man hard at work in this SAW PIT.

The water in the pool is maintained from two springs, one of which supplies all the needs of the house and your tea! This lovely fresh spring water then flows down the valley and finally runs into the Helford. At one time fresh water trout used the stream, the pool, and the Helford. However, pollution and mink have more or less put paid to fresh water trout, but there are still some fresh water eels, lurking in the mud at the bottom of the pool, and a heron is not averse to a tasty breakfast.

It is difficult to appreciate now that the valley was almost inaccessible with no proper paths, just overgrown and wild as it always had been. The entire winter of 79/80 was spent in clearing and preparing the Lower Valley Path, well over 400 yards long. The first plantings were made in April 1980 in the area opposite the Middle Bridge, and after some 20 large trees were cut down; the other two bridges were constructed at the same time, in order to view this delightful stream, overhung with trees and its banks clad with ferns and moss, babbling down over the many rills to the Helford. During the winter of 80/81 the major construction got under way with a big bite being made into the valleyside, in order to dig out and create two level areas for plantings, a complex now known as the Folly, where stands the Sun-dial, set in inch-thick slabs of Delabole Slate mid-way between the two flat beds faced with 7 tons of Serpentine Stone, approached by three large granite steps, with granite groins and mushrooms. All this lot, with the plants and trees, being manhandled down from the Farmyard - mostly in monsoon conditions! - with an Upper Path surmounted by a Bus Shelter - a FOLLY all right!

1981/82 saw the creation of the RAINBOW PATH ascending the valleyside from the back of the Folly to join up with the Top Valley Path - this Rainbow Path landscaped in such a way as to give maximum viewing over the valley and river to the Northern side of the Helford, with rustic handrails set up because of its steepness. All the plantings on either side of this path were carried out in the Spring of 82.

During the Winter of 82/83 the top end of the valley was planted up, together with completing the plantings of the large Rhododendrons between the Lower Valley Path and the stream, entailing much cutting back of the trees.

During 84/85 the Top Look-out Shelter was knocked up, and the new Long Path from the top of the Rainbow right down to join up with the Folly and the Woodland Path, which goes down behind the Bridges area, passing the fine big oak, estimated to be about 240 years old. Also recently constructed is the Waterway and small pool to the left of Doodes Lane, together with a lot more restoration to the pool itself.

The Trelean Valley Garden was formally opened by Elizabeth, Viscountess Falmouth, in May 1983, accompanied by Lord Falmouth, the Lord Lieutenant of the County. To mark the occasion Lady Falmouth planted a Robinia FRISIA tree in the Farmyard, using a spade previously handled by the Queen Mother when planting a tree, to mark her opening of the new DUCHY Hospital, Truro.

Gardens are not made in a hurry, and some are never made at all, but a start is a good beginning; nevertheless the real charm of TRELEAN lies in its natural beauty as you walk down to the river and back up to the VALLEY.

GEORGE WITHERWICK

To return to those early days at 'Trelean', one of our first calls was from Peter London, who had taken on the job of raising money in this part of Cornwall for a private hospital. The county had no such establishment, all medical care being available only through the NHS. The whole project was presided over by the Viscountess Falmouth of Tregothnan, a lady whose horticultural knowledge had greatly impressed me when I had met her previously.

Peter London soon got to the crux of the matter and asked if I would contribute to the new hospital at Truro. When I agreed to do so and mentioned the sum I was prepared to donate, he seemed quite taken aback. Little did he know of my hatred for the union-dominated Health Service and that this was a way in which I could do something positive to restore standards of medical treatment to what they were before the profession was nationalised. I also said that if no other arrangements had been made to landscape the grounds, I would be happy to do so, and to offer my services as Honorary Consulting Dental Surgeon to the hospital.

In due course he arranged for me to visit the four-acre site. On arrival I had a bit of a shock when I saw the deep pit that had been dug to lower the single-storey building below the path of the prevailing Westerlies. The combination of high wind exposure and a clay sub-soil for planting did nothing to boost my confidence.

When planting commenced in March my worst fears were confirmed. Here undoubtedly was the windiest place I had ever tried to cultivate. The wind whistled and howled; sometimes a full gale, never less than a cool, stiff breeze. On several occasions it was too strong to walk against, and I feared for the survival of my plants. Somehow the lie of the land on its western boundary tended to funnel the Westerlies into a kind of wind tunnel - conditions that made careful choice of plants of paramount importance.

I was glad I had ordered the hundred pounds worth of selected trees from a nursery near Aberdeen, on the principle that they would be fully hardened in that location. These were augmented by a lorry-load of biggish conifers from Trelean to go into the bare soil at the front of the hospital. Close by was a small, round bed immediately opposite the front entrance, and here I planted a 12-foot Aesculus Neglecta Erythroblastos as a centre-piece. Surrounding it would be five large Pieris Forrestii 'Wakehurst' shrubs to complement the brilliant shrimp-pink of the Chestnut's emerging leaves. Beyond these, and forming the perimeter, were eight dozen primroses from

Trelean.

On the day before the Queen Mother's visit on April 10th, we faced a serious problem with the weather. Heavy rain driven by a vicious half-gale persisted, but at four o'clock I could delay no longer. The *pieris* that I had carefully nurtured for weeks had been taken to Truro in a horse-box, kindly driven by Bill Gillmore, on the previous day. Stuck in the middle of this bed, soaked to the skin already, I gave the word to Andrew, my sole helper, to bring the precious plants to me from the horse-box, one by one, a distance of some twenty yards that must have felt like a mile to him as he faced the wind.

No sooner had we commenced this final stage than the wind increased its intensity, and the rain lashed my face as though to flay the skin from it. I had managed to get three of the *pieris* planted when, on turning to signal for the next one, I saw through the curtain of rain that the wind was blowing with such force as to strip the delicate red shoots clean off the branches.

At this point I was seized with utter despair. A violent urge to abandon the whole thing and hurl the spade straight through the glass door of the entrance foyer boiled up in me. I raged at the elements and cursed the impulse that committed me to this madness of thinking that my gardening skills could triumph over this hostile environment.

Even stronger than my anger was the determination to complete what I had started. Grimly I set to again with my spade, and lo and behold! within minutes the wind dropped and the rain ceased. At about 6.30 the clouds drew aside to reveal the evening sun that illuminated the beauty I had created. Not for the first time in my life, I felt that somebody up there had heeded my despair. I do believe that if you strive hard enough, fate will give you a helping hand just when defeat seems inevitable.

The opening ceremony was performed next day by the Queen Mother with her inimitable charm, and I was proud to help her plant the Acer Crimson King I had chosen. The spade was one that had been used by her daughter, Queen Elizabeth in 1977 at Roussillon Barracks, and I took the opportunity to offer the Queen Mother the traditional gift, in this instance a framed photograph of one of her residences, the Castle of Mey, recalling for me the 1938 honeymoon that had taken Audrey and me to Scotland.

Unhappily that tree did not thrive. Each winter the rough winds cut it back to such a degree that four years after planting, it was 2½ ft. less in height than it was originally! Now this tree, related to the

Sycamore, is no delicate subject! but I had to dig it up and transplant it in the vortex behind the hospital on the lee side, where I hope it will survive.

Other trees - Leylandii, Scots Pine, Larch, Silver Birch - all were mutilated or killed by the savage conditions. Macrocarpa, hardy elsewhere, is among the very few trees that have any chance, but only the Golden varieties such as Lutea or Donards Gold seem to be able to withstand the onslaught of those winds, salt-laden when their velocity exceeds about 60 mph. Of the one hundred pounds worth of trees I planted at the Duchy Hospital, only three at the time of writing have survived. It has still not been possible to get a hedge to grow on the boundary. The original one has been replanted no fewer than four times and is probably a lost cause now.

Sometimes one's best is not enough.

One of my prime objectives in coming to Trelean by the Helford River was to create from scratch a Valley garden. In many ways it has been a frustrating exercise, far more so than making my garden in Surrey which was twice the size as regards plantable area. Due to the extremes of weather conditions on the Lizard my losses of plants in twelve years have been twice as many as during the thirty years in Surrey, including that terrible drought of 1976. Even in a valley, the wind here is devastating. There are places on the East side of the Lizard which are blasted wildernesses of plant life, not helped by the phenomenon of autumn. Due to the warmth of the sea all round this finger of land, lush growth persists right up to Christmas. But January brings the cruel east wind, usually laden with salt and frost, and all this new tender growth is blasted and seared. In January 1987 with a 65 mph velocity, this wind with 18° of frost and driving fine, dry snow killed five 30 ft. Acacias, known as Mimosa trees, eight 30ft Eucalyptus and cut others back to ground level in this valley. Everywhere I went showed the same ravages of wind and frost, especially to the delicate palms, those well-established trees that usually thrive in the supposed 'Riviera of England'. In the famous Tresco Gardens in the Isles of Scilly there was utter devastation, and I get the feeling that nothing garden-wise will ever be the same again.

One wonders if the Gulf Stream has been diverted or undergone a drop in temperature for all this to happen, as we were also cut off from civilisation for five days with drifts of snow five feet high, as fine and dry as snuff, all on the Lizard Peninsula, the furthest point south on the UK mainland. No wonder the Helston Packet considered the visitation the worst in living memory. My observations made over the past few years have convinced me that the most stable part of Cornwall from a horticultural point of view is the area between Falmouth and Truro. Everywhere else is too near the coast and suffers from the wind. The Lizard is hit by a greater velocity of east wind than any other piece of Cornwall but gets on average more sun-hours than any other place in the county. Furthermore the weather on the Lizard is often different from that generally prevailing in the south-west as I have often noticed a change in the wind direction by observation of the cloud movement, and forecast a similar change of weather pattern (at any rate to myself) often up to 24 hours before the penny drops at Bracknell. What the eye sees and one's senses feel is more acute and reliable than the act of sitting inside away from it all, reading tapes and looking at computers.

In 1983 the Valley garden was opened to the public by Viscountess Falmouth, the proceeds of the small entrance fee going to charity. I am happy to say that from small beginnings, the number of visitors annually has steadily increased. This has not meant that I could stand back and rest on my laurels (or perhaps I should say "spade"!). There is always something to do, on top of those routine household chores that some people wistfully imagine they will magically escape from on retirement. Since we moved here in February 1979, my wife has not spent a single day away from the place, and I only a week to visit my brother-in-law in the West Riding of Yorkshire. Sadly he is no longer with us, like so many other dear friends and relatives.

Audrey and I celebrated our Golden Wedding Anniversary in 1988, following which I received a charming reply from the Queen Mother's lady-in-waiting, thanking me for my letter and copy of "In a Cornish Valley." This little booklet of 43 pages is in the form of a 12-month diary, covering the period October 1981 to September 1982 at Trelean. I felt that the Queen Mother, as interested as others of the Royal Family in the principle of conservation, would also note that the proceeds of sale were donated to Churchtown Farm, the Spastic Society's Field Studies Centre at Lanlivery.

By the end of 1988, Audrey had developed the symptoms of Alzheimer's disease, and since then has been increasingly dependent on my constant attendance to her needs. I now have daily help Monday to Friday, which frees me for other tasks but is an expensive business. Well intentioned as these helpers are, there seems to be a shortage of mature people. The younger ones have great difficulty in communicating with a person of 80, whose interests are quite different. However, one is grateful for any help.

Looking back on all this now in my 80th year, I know I shall recall names and incidents that should have been recorded. During the past few years my life has been in turmoil due to Audrey contracting Alzheimer's. Until you have actually lived with it as a 'carer' you cannot by any stretch of imagination even begin to understand the devastating effect that comes between you and your loved one. It is indeed well named 'a living death'. Nevertheless a handful of good people have given me hope, strength and encouragement to carry on. Olga Pickering is one who has made half a dozen visits from Sussex to give moral support; Betty Wilson, a pillar of strength to uplift, listen and help not only me but Audrey, more than anyone else - there cannot be many like her in her goodness of heart. Also Charmaine Pearson and Trevor McCabe, our vicar, both of these having suffered themselves in a similar vein, have been most kind and understanding: Jean Marcus has constantly used her kindness in long telephone conversations of goodwill, as have Paul Marcus and Ian Wort and his charming nurse-wife Anne. Oh yes, Mary Foister even counsels me from Cambridge with her nice sense of humour and with a voice over the phone booming as gently as a bittern, and that dear lady at Tregothnan has, in spite of her trials and tribulations, given me and Audrey much pleasure from her company and understanding. Yet there are many others, not least Norman Truscott who gives so much help for so little.

Other staunch helpers were Dick Davies and Margaret Burford, together with John Anderson and Bridget Marsden. Then there is courageous Doug Sale fighting to live, yet so happy to help others. Lest we forget, four Master Craftsmen, Howard Stephens, Frank Birchall, John Valender and Michael Davidson, so willing in their support - bless 'em all.

EPILOGUE

Looking back over these pages, I am aware of certain omissions. In particular, I should like to expand on the experiences of more than half a century's active gardening, but that would require a further book to do full justice to. There are some other matters, however, that I can squeeze into the brief miscellany that follows.

My life-span has encompassed more radical changes affecting this country than at any similar period in our history. Radio and tele-communications, mechanised transport, air travel, modern drugs, now part of our everyday lives, were unknown or in the infancy of their development when I was born. Two World Wars and their aftermath brought about a social and socialist revolution without bloodshed but with devastating effects on the world I grew up in.

One of the casualties has been the slow erosion of civility or common courtesy, looked upon by many of the younger generation as servility in an age when Jack believes himself as good as his master, to resurrect a time-worn phrase.

Courtesy between the wars implied a respect for the other person and manifested itself in many ways, not least in the doffing of the hat or the touching of the cap. Every adult, man or woman, was considered ill-dressed on the street or at outdoor functions without a hat, which brings me to the first of my afterthoughts.

My own first post-war hat, a splendid Trilby by Christey, was part of my demobilisation oufit and went beautifully with the overcoat I was presented with at the time and which disappeared from a Cornish pub, as related earlier. This hat took to the air in the late 'forties when I was changing trains at London Bridge for the Underground. One of those sudden gusts of wind that spring out unannounced from those tunnels caught it and whipped it away on to the line. It went slap into the middle well conveying the electrified rail, and for a moment I was nonplussed. Then, with only one thought in mind, to retrieve my precious hat, I jumped on to the line and ran to where I had seen it land. There, to my amazement, I found four other hats, all trapped in that same spot!

I duly captured them all, pushed each one into the other, and clambered back on to the platform with my spoils. I had heard the shouts of a coloured porter, and as I ran off I could hear him in hot pursuit. Making for the nearest escalator, I went up it at high speed, followed by his furious yells, and once at the top, doubled back on the down-travelling stairway, sitting on the stairs below the banister rail so as to be out of sight from the other side.

The ruse worked. He must have assumed I had merged with the other anonymous travellers, and I was able to resume my journey, the richer for four hats. None of them fitted when I tried them on, but at least I had retrieved my own. As for the porter, I sometimes wonder whether his concern was for my safety or an expression of his frustration at losing a valuable perk!

. . . . . .

Another droll though unrelated incident occurred shortly after, when I had reopened my pre-war surgery and was forced into joining the NHS. Sometime around the sixth or seventh month of the new regime, when I wondered how I could continue to cope with the pressure, an idea struck me. Why not seek work again in one of the hospitals? It would break up the week, take me into a less frenzied working environment, and give me a day or two to collect my wits.

The current issue of the British Dental Journal had just arrived, and there on the back page was an advertisement that appeared to offer just what I was looking for. A hospital at Banstead, near Epsom, needed a dentist for one session weekly. I thought I knew just where it was, and promptly wrote off. In due course, I was asked to attend for interview.

On the appointed day, I was running late, as usual - twenty minutes by the time I had turned into the hospital driveway. As soon as I read the sign-board I realised I was at the wrong hospital. In something of a sweat by now, I regained the main road, and there was lucky enough to spot a woman wheeling a pram who gave me precise directions. Twenty minutes later, I was at hospital, wondering whether it was worth going in. Then I reasoned that being forty minutes late could be explained away by pressure of work, and having parked the car I announced myself at Reception and was shown into a waiting-room.

175

To my amazement it was full of hopeful applicants. There must have been forty but only one I knew, a Harley Street man called Allen. He had been in already and primed me with the questions asked, so that when I went in I felt confident.

The interview went like a house on fire, and when everybody had been seen, I was not surprised when Allen and I were asked to remain for a second interview.

Allen went in to say his piece, but came out looking despondent. "It's yours on a plate," he told me as I passed him on the way into the committee room. "I made a bloody mess of it."

My second interview turned out to be little more than a formality. I was well qualified for the post, I could name the day of attendance most suitable to me, and I would receive their formal confirmation in the morning. If there was anything I felt I needed for the surgery, it would be obtained, etc.

I was congratulating myself, with my hand on the door handle ready to leave, when Madam Chairman spoke from the committee table. "By the way, Mr. Witherwick, I forgot to ask why you put in for this appointment."

I turned back to the committee and explained my views on the NHS, the lowering of standards and the difficulties of treating such an avalanche of patients. I finished by saying. "If I don't get out of my surgery mid-week, I shall end up in a mental institution."

Madam Chairman's face changed as I watched. The benevolent expression was replaced by a distinct tightening of the lips and hardening of the features. An awesome silence pervaded the room. The Chairman spoke.

"That will be quite enough, Mr. Witherwick. Good day to you."

Somehow I stumbled from that room. I got into the car, searching my mind for what had gone wrong. I had answered all questions properly and honestly. What could have brought about this bewildering change of fortune? I drove to the entrance gate in a daze and stopped by the large notice board. Yes, I had been to the right hospital. No doubt about that. There was the name, bold and clear. I then examined the bottom part of the board which was half-covered by vegetation, making the partly concealed words hard to discern. When I was able to read their message, all became clear. It said: "THIS IS A MENTAL INSTITUTION."

. . . . . .

The carnage of World War II accelerated research and

development of surgical techniques and anaesthetics. 'General Anaesthetic' was, in my youth, a term which put the fear of death into most people, especially those who suffered from some complaint which would need an operation in hospital and thereby require an anaesthetic. My father for instance suffered discomfort, inconvenience and severe pain nearly all his life, from haemorrhoids. I tried many times to persuade him to have an operation, extolling the virtues of the new methods of anaesthesia but no, he would not do it, and it was an embolism or blood clot which probably arose from this condition that caused his death within ten minutes of the heart attack.

The main reason for the fear of anaesthetic was due to the currency of such sombre announcements as ...... "it is regretted that Mr.Jones died in hospital from or under the anaesthetic." Whether this was strictly true I really don't know. Perhaps the word 'anaesthetic' covered a multitude of sins, medical, surgical or otherwise - a bit like today when the doctor, unable to diagnose the source of your problem, states that you are suffering from a 'virus', quite often specific to the area of the doctor's practice.

When I embarked upon my hospital training, chloroform was on the way out. Certainly I was not trained on it, although my medical colleagues were. In fact for many years after qualification the average GP one called in from courtesy to give a dental anaesthetic to his patient had no idea of how to begin. Many a time I gave the anaesthetic to the patient and left the doctor to hold the nose piece on, with the apparatus running, whilst I got on and carried out the necessary operation. When I first worked with the now defunct London County Council before the war, I was doing two gas sessions a week, involving perhaps up to a dozen cases, and it was most often the inability of the anaesthetist, i.e. a GP to put the patient to sleep, which caused these sessions to run late.

At the Edinburgh Dental Hospital in the 'thirties the general anaesthetic was nitrous oxide (gas), oxygen and ethyl chloride, the latter added in small quantities to the mixture as it was inhaled through a mask which covered the nose and the mouth of the patient. As not a few of these patients came to the hospital from the Grass Market district, courage bolstered with liquid refreshment and topped up in the waiting room from small bottles kept within their apparel, we were often hard put to anaesthetise these gentlemen at all, and liberal use of the ethyl chloride well above the prescribed limit had to be resorted to.

I will not enlarge upon scenes which often resembled a five-ale-bar skirmish, with five or six white-coated stalwarts trying to subdue an exuberant blowing whale of a man trying to break out of the ring of flying arms intent on enmeshing him. It was, of course, the alcohol that inhibited the nitrous oxide from rendering the patient unconscious, and it was then necessary to re-commence the procedure, this time slipping a strong belt across the man's abdomen to strap him into the chair. When the operation was over, which it had to be within a matter of four to five minutes, the scene again would become quite lively, with the added flow of expletives about our parentage and the poor patient neither drunk nor sober but half unconscious, with a mouthful of blood, unable to comprehend where or what had happened to him, the alcohol previously imbibed interfering with his conscious recovery.

By the time I left hospital the standard anaesthetic was nitrous oxide and oxygen given with face mask having a nasal attachment for continuous and prolonged operations, with the intravenous injections just being introduced. Within six months I was in London and operating in some of the major General Hospitals in 1939.

In London the general anaesthetic was more advanced, as I soon discovered. The intravenous method was in general use as the predominant and fundamental anaesthetic and continued in this form for most of the war years. The main trouble then was the possibility of respiratory inhibition with some of the early solutions used such as Evipan, and I certainly experienced several narrow escapes between presiding over a corpse or a living patient using this anaesthetic solution.

When I returned to civilian practice after my six years in the RAFVR, anaesthetics had taken another step forward. The massive time of recovery from the average operation that patients had formerly to endure was, with the new products, much reduced. For dental use, instead of using a normal intravenous injection, a small or reduced dose was injected, just sufficient for the patient to lose consciousness, after which the anaesthetic was switched to nitrous oxide and oxygen, using the nasal inhalation method. The dentist was thus able to undertake his operation which, on average, was of short duration and the patient was quickly able to recover either in the recovery room or waiting room. In hospital, long recovery was no problem as you were bedded down and not expected to walk out of the place and return home.

This was the procedure in my practice from 1952 onwards. I had, on returning to it in 1947, resorted to the general anaesthetic. However, this proved so frustrating, culminating in one near fatality in my surgery due to the incompetence of the particular General Practitioner, that I resolved not to expose myself to that risk again.

Under the NHS rules I was liable to harsh penalties simply because it was my Practice, and as its Principal part of the blame could be levied on me for the death of a patient. The fact that a medically qualified person had administered the anaesthetic did not absolve me; it was my machine and it could have been faulty. If I had given the anaesthetic myself without a medical practitioner present, then it was all my fault. Many a time I actually gave the anaesthetic and operated as well, with the doctor present more as an insurance against the unfortunate occurrence of death.

So, in 1952 my association with Dr. John Gordon, anaesthetist, began, and continued harmoniously until I gave up my practice. He was an anaesthetist on the circuit of major General Hospitals from Kingston-upon-Thames across to Croydon, and assisted me every two weeks for my general anaesthetic session when we usually dealt with at least six cases within an hour, using two surgeries, a recovery room and three nurses. The anaesthetic procedure was a small intravenous injection and then transference to nitrous oxide and oxygen given by nasal inhalation - quick operative procedure, quick recovery and the patient into the recovery room. In nearly twenty years and hundreds of cases there was never an occasion to cause either of us a moment of lost sleep.

. . . . . .

The most obvious change I have witnessed is in the development of the motor-car and the growth of road traffic. I have been a keen motorist since I acquired a licence in 1928 and have driven untold thousands of miles since. I did not wear a seat-belt until it became illegal not to "belt up", and I am proud to say that I have never had an accident requiring any endorsement of my licence.

It is well known that early cars were generally more strongly built than present ones though much less reliable. I can recall a frightening experience at the age of fifteen when I was a passenger in a Bull-Nosed Morris driven by my late sister, then a superior eighteen-year-old. It was an open two-seater which I had already learnt to drive in many hours of practice in a four-acre field. I had no faith in her driving ability and had to suffer her "Stop telling me what to do, George."

Driving through Hull and wishing to turn off the main road in the city centre, she put her hand out of the window (no traffic indicators then) and shot across the path of a bus to turn left into a side-street, causing the bus to make an emergency stop to avoid us. When I pointed out her awful error of judgment she blandly said: "You should have put your hand out. You knew we were turning down here. I was just waving to someone I knew on the pavement."

Another incident in Hull, driving with her in the same car, was even more worrying. We came to a five-road junction controlled by a policeman on point-duty, when Enid decided she needed to turn. She swung the wheel on to full lock, the car heeling over on two wheels, and the steering promptly seized. Desperately she tried to straighten it, but it was jammed solid. When I tried to grab the wheel she knocked my hand away, and with both her hands on the wheel, half-rose in the seat as though to pull the wheel off. That is exactly what happened! There she was, clutching the useless wheel to her bosom, the car out of control, and heading staight for the pavement with its shops and pedestrians.

At that point she really panicked and tried to brake, but instead, her foot hit the accelerator. Fate then appeared to take a hand. We found ourselves pointing towards the only object between us and the shop-fronts, a Corporation lamp-standard, and this we hit with great force, coming to a halt with an almighty jolt.

The massive structure of the old Morris had absorbed sufficient of the impact to enable us to climb out unscathed. We were fortunate indeed, but the whole point of the anecdote is that this same panic reaction - jabbing the accelerator instead of the brake - is one of the most common causes of road accidents with inexperienced drivers. yet it could be avoided by making the brake pedal operate with the accelerator, with one pedal serving both functions. Impossible? It's been done. During my RAFVR service I met a man who had developed such a system. He was a fellow officer, Flt. Lt. Martin, and was only too pleased to demonstrate the car he had converted.

It felt strange at first, but with the vast space of the airfield perimeter track to ourselves, I soon became accustomed. The pedal gave progressive acceleration in response to increased pressure, just as any other car accelerator will. Pressed sharply down, the clever linkage operated the hydraulics, and on came the brakes. We had a marvellous time, practising emergency stops and zipping along at up to sixty miles an hour - no mean speed then, when even a Bentley cruised at little more than eighty.

Why was this ingenious device never taken up and developed by a manufacturer? Who knows? Perhaps we're not as advanced as we like to imagine we are.

. . . . . .

While the development of the motor-car was a gradual process, that of air transport appeared to take a giant step forward in the early to mid 'fifties. The proximity of Farnborough to our Runforld home on the outskirts of Farnham and Aldershot did little to disturb our peace until one Saturday afternoon when I was taking a few minutes rest on the edge of my large wooden wheelbarrow, on the lawn at the front of the house. Without warning, the blast of a tremendous explosion knocked me off my perch and shattered my wits.

My first thought was that it came from a cottage some three hundred yards down the road. I rushed off to give what aid I could, and found the two maiden ladies shaking with fear in their tiny living room. There was no sign of damage, and none of us could find an explanation. There had been none of the prior rumblings that herald a storm, and the whole thing was inexplicable.

Soon after this, I was one of a little group standing at the local bus-stop at Thrumblands Corner when another massive blast shook us all. Again, nobody had the slightest idea of the cause.

The Farnham Herald printed letters from readers who complained of ceilings cracked or partly brought down, shattered windows, wrecked greenhouses. Our local MP made enquiries through the usual channels, eliciting no response. The bangs continued until, under mounting pressure from constituents, a Question was put down in Parliament, which by its nature required a direct answer. Only then did the Minister for Defence acknowledge that the disturbances were caused by "sonic booms" created by supersonic aircraft breaking the sound barrier.

It was eventually decreed that such incidents should be limited to the period of the Farnborough Airshow - an obvious venue for demonstrating Britain's advanced technology in this field. The pilots concerned were adept in their timing, breaking the sound barrier as they came in from the sea and crossed the coast at Selsey Bill, so that the sound wave and boom would hit the Airshow on the North side of the Hog's Back, causing the thousands attending to jump out of their skins. After three or four years, the novelty was outweighed by the annoyance of those in the path of the nuisance, and the practice discontinued.

$\cdot \cdot \cdot \cdot \cdot \cdot$

Enthusiasm for a hobby or righteous cause has sometimes overruled my native common sense, as when I read an article in the "Daily Telegraph" in respect of a Lady who had undertaken to restore and rehabilitate Burghley House in Lincolnshire. Lord Burghley, the famous British athlete who won glory and Olympic medals during the 'thirties, was one of my boyhood heroes. Fired with the desire to help with this project, I wrote to the Lady offering my services in the event of her wishing to put the gardens to rights.

In due course I received a nice letter in reply, but it was her last sentence that brought me up short. It went something like this: "...... as for the Estate grounds, a man called Brown laid them out in a rather Capable way some time ago."

I think this rounds things off nicely.